# Transfiguration and Hope

# Transfiguration and Hope

A Conversation across Time and Space

D. GREGORY VAN DUSSEN
Foreword by Larry R. Baird

WIPF & STOCK · Eugene, Oregon

TRANSFIGURATION AND HOPE
A Conversation across Time and Space

Wipf & Stock
An Imprint of Wipf and Stock Publishers
199 W. 8th Ave., Suite 3
Eugene, OR 97401

www.wipfandstock.com

PAPERBACK ISBN: 978-1-5326-5453-4
HARDCOVER ISBN: 978-1-5326-5454-1
EBOOK ISBN: 978-1-5326-5455-8

Manufactured in the U.S.A.                                         09/11/18

To my wife, Jackie, our family, and all who
have encouraged me along the way.

# Contents

# Foreword

WHEN I WAS A child my father, who was an accomplished photographer, presented programs in the area schools and churches. His programs were called "Learning to See." He would begin the series with a pastoral scene such as a wooded area in the distance. He would then move in photographically getting closer and closer to individual trees, and then onward focusing on their leaves, individual birds, and even minute insect life. His title was appropriate because he was teaching people to see what they might otherwise miss or be unaware of in their lives. Later, in adulthood, after college and seminary, and becoming a pastor, I always thought of "Learning to See" when I was preaching on or teaching about The Transfiguration. The Transfiguration was God's gift to us to enable us to learn to see Jesus' identity and part of his nature we might otherwise fail to see.

Some people, like my father, have the gift of enabling us to see beyond the everyday and beyond what we might consider ordinary. Such a person is my colleague, and good friend D. Gregory VanDussen.

When Greg asked me to do some preliminary reading and review his work entitled *Transfiguration and Hope* I agreed thinking that having been a pastor preacher for over forty years, I would be prepared to work through familiar territory. Much to my surprise and delight it took me only a few chapters to realize Greg was taking us on a journey far deeper than I had been accustomed to travelling in understanding the significance and import of the Transfiguration.

This volume is a rich depository of careful Biblical and theological research into the meaning of the Transfiguration and the hope it generates for individual Christians as well as the whole Christian community. It is in my opinion a great contribution to enrich our understanding and application of this sometimes-neglected tenet of our faith.

It is with great excitement that I will reread and utilize this book in my own study, devotions, and sermon preparation. It would be my prayer that many will use this work to broaden their understanding of the faith and enable them to share the treasures therein. As our author says, hope sustains when we discover "a purpose that runs deeper and lasts longer than any other involvement, one that is solidly rooted in God." Such is the hope in Transfiguration that helps us truly " learn to see."

**Larry R. Baird**
Clarence, NY

# Acknowledgments

I VERY MUCH APPRECIATE those who have, through conversation, writing, and example, lived and taught the reality of transfiguration and hope.

My thanks to all who have assisted me throughout this project. Special thanks to Larry Baird and to my wife, Jackie, for their helpful comments on each chapter, and to Matthew Wimer and the editorial staff at Wipf and Stock.

# Introduction

O what a foretaste of glory divine
—"Blessed Assurance," *The United Methodist Hymnal*

The spiritual path is a journey towards perfection, the route to which is constant
spiritual growth.
—Pope Senouda III, *Characteristics of the Spiritual Path*

He who in such amazing grace descended to make our lost cause his own, ascended
in accomplishment of his task, elevating man into union and communion with the
life of God.
—Thomas F. Torrance, *Incarnation*

We dwell on unimportant things, and we carelessly skip over the most important thing
of all.
—Thomas à Kempis, *The Imitation of Christ*

My Lord and my God, the joy and hope of my heart
I cannot know you fully in this life,
but let me grow here in your knowledge and love
so that in the world to come
I may find the fullness of love and knowledge.
Let me live here in joyful hope, so that I may come one day
to the fulfillment of all hope and joy.
— Eamon Duffy, *Heart in Pilgrimage*

Introduction

I HAVE ALWAYS ENJOYED reflecting and preaching on the transfiguration. The story itself is amazing, full of mystery, its full meaning not immediately apparent. There have been times, in fact, when I have come to the end of one of the transfiguration accounts and wondered what on earth I had just read. Like iconographers and painters over the centuries, I have tried to imagine that mountaintop scene, with its cast of Old and New Testament characters and a radiance the evangelists struggled to describe:

> His face shone like the sun, and his clothes became as white as the light. (Matt 17:2 NIV)

> His clothes became dazzling white, whiter than anyone in the world could bleach them. (Mark 9:3 NIV)

> As he was praying, the appearance of his face changed, and his clothes became as bright as a flash of lightning. (Luke 9:29 NIV)

The story in the first three Gospels, and its image in traditional iconography, inspires a fascination that grows over time. Its importance becomes clearer and more compelling when seen through a broad range of Christian traditions. For this reason, I have looked to Protestant, Eastern Orthodox, Anglican, Roman Catholic, and Oriental Orthodox sources for interpretation and reflection on the transfiguration itself and the hope it offers for human destiny. I write from my own Wesleyan tradition within that larger, ecumenical context, much as John and Charles Wesley wrote within and beyond their own Anglican tradition. My intent is a conversation across time and space on the transfiguration and hope.

The exploration offered here makes no attempt to provide a geography of heaven or a chronology for the last days—"an exercise in futility that has tempted too many Christian preachers over the centuries."[1] The transfiguration leads us to deeper and more lasting insights into the mystery of God's purpose and plan in transforming human life and creation itself. The transfiguration represents not so much a single, cataclysmic event, but a new heaven and a new earth, starting with the restoration of the image and likeness of God in humanity.

Nor will we try to decide whether Mount Tabor or Mount Hermon is the most likely site for the transfiguration. Tradition, at least from the time of Cyril of Jerusalem (fourth century AD), clearly favors Tabor, while the context in the Gospels seems to suggest Hermon. What matters most is the event itself and its meaning for us, though certainly something of the

1. Egan, *Book of Hours*, 176.

power of the event has long come through to pilgrims who have visited the traditional site on Tabor.[2]

The world has seen too much of people and nations pursuing their own selfish and short-sighted ends, and leaving destruction and disappointment in their wake. The transfiguration looks far beyond human wisdom and ambition to what God is accomplishing in his new creation. And since God has given the church—in spite of its all-too-human foibles—a vital role in that restoration, "the transfiguration is the church's symbol of hope . . ."[3]

Mack Stokes says that "there are really two levels of Christian hope. One is the hope for a better life on earth. The other is the hope for a marvelous life in that new realm that we call the kingdom of Heaven."[4] This distinction is helpful, but not ultimate, since God's kingdom spans both worlds. Like grace, Christian hope undergirds the whole panorama of life. Hope extends to the height and depth of this life, and, most importantly, to the endless expanses of eternity. Nothing, no matter how devastating, can erase that kind of hope.

The transfiguration of Christ and its meaning for humanity is an intriguing and powerful story and symbol of hope. In this story, Peter, James, and John, three disciples who figure prominently in the Gospels, climb what they would one day call "the sacred mountain," and there see Jesus in a way they had never seen him before (2 Pet 1:18 NIV). This was neither a slight transformation, nor one for which they were at all prepared.

They saw light shining out from within him in a way that was far more than metaphorical. They witnessed at close range something of the mystery of God incarnate. That would have been spectacular enough, but it was just the beginning. They saw Jesus talking with two men long dead, Moses and Elijah, key figures in the Old Testament pilgrimage of Israel, prophets who spoke with Jesus concerning what lay ahead for him and, consequently, for his followers. They heard the voice of God speaking a word about his Son, and exhorting them to "listen to him" (Luke 9:35 NIV). They had no idea how to respond, and when one of them tried, his words made little sense.

Clearly these disciples were privileged to see Jesus more profoundly than ever before, even if they could not understand the meaning of what they saw. But there was still more. They were also seeing what God had in store for the people he had created in his own image, once that image

2. Davies, *Pilgrimage*, 227; Sumption, *Age of Pilgrimage*, 127.

3. McGuckin, *Transfiguration of Christ in Scripture*, 133.

4. Stokes, *Person to Person*, 164.

Introduction

is restored in Christ. They were seeing themselves as they could be under the leadership of Jesus and the transforming power of the Spirit. As we witness their experience through Scripture, we can begin to see ourselves transformed as well. "In the end, it is as much about their [the disciples'] transfiguration . . . as it is about Jesus' transformation."[5]

> The whole design of God was to restore man to his image, and raise him from the ruins of his fall; in a word, to make him perfect; to blot out all his sins, purify his soul, and fill him with holiness, so that no unholy temper, evil desire, or impure affection or passion shall either lodge, or have any being within him; this and only this is true religion, or Christian perfection.[6]

Adam Clarke's very Wesleyan description of Christian perfection is exactly what God's metamorphosis was designed to produce. And Vladimir Lossky notes, "Human nature must undergo a change; it must be more and more transfigured by grace in the way of sanctification, which has a range which is not only spiritual but also bodily—and hence cosmic."[7] As Michael Ramsey put it, "the perfect vision will be only when our transformation is complete."[8] Bishop Scott Jones says, "The ultimate goal of salvation for each person is the restoration of the image of God. Thus, the process of sanctifying grace leads believers to grow toward the point where they are made fully righteous."[9] The Cistercian monk Michael Casey writes about transfiguration and becoming "like him [Christ]" (1 John 3:2 NIV): "This is the goal of our existence. It is towards this that our journey leads."[10] "The goal is transformation," says David Long, "and in all this we are dependent upon the grace of God to become who he created us to be."[11]

Frederica Mathewes-Green makes the classic connection between Jesus' transfiguration and that of his people: "At his transfiguration, Christ's 'face shone like the sun' (Mt. 17:2). This is our destiny, too."[12] John's First Letter includes the mysterious and hope-filled promise that one day, "when Christ appears, we shall be like him, for we shall see him as he is" (1 John

5. Lee, *Transfiguration*, 2.
6. Clarke, *Christian Theology*, 184.
7. Lossky, *Mystical Theology*, 18.
8. Ramsey, *Glory of God*, 53.
9. Jones, *United Methodist Doctrine*, 210.
10. Casey, *Fully Human, Fully Divine*, 197.
11. Long, *Quest for Holiness*, xii.
12. Mathewes-Green, *Jesus Prayer*, 98.

3:2 NIV). The transfiguration offers a glimpse and image of "as he is." In his commentary on 1 John, B. F. Westcott says "our likeness to the Lord will be a likeness to His glorified being, which will hereafter be shewn, though as yet we cannot understand what it is." Even without complete understanding, Westcott says, "The image in which we were made will then be consummated in the likeness to which it was the divine purpose that we should attain. . . . This likeness of man redeemed and perfected to God is the likeness of the creature reflecting the glory of the Creator."[13] I. Howard Marshall comments on the same passage:

> John does not state explicitly in what new ways we shall be like Jesus at the Parousia. But we may assume that the privileges which we now enjoy in a trial manner will then be ours fully and completely. Not only so, but we may also recollect that our hope is to see Jesus in his glory (Jn 17:1, 5, 24) and therefore our hope is to share his glory, a hope that is clearly expressed by Paul (Rm. 8:17–19; Phil. 3:21; Col. 3:4). The process of glorification, already begun here and now in the lives of believers (2 Cor. 3:18), will reach completion.[14]

We humans may be content with limited, gradual change that falls far short of complete transformation, but as we look to our destiny in Christ, a very different picture emerges. God sees more in us than we see in ourselves. He sees the fulfillment of his original purpose for our lives: the restoration in us of his own image. "We are made for heaven, our ultimate home, which one day will be a 'new heaven and a new earth,' as part of God's recreation of the world."[15] We become who we were created to be "by reaching out into infinity" and finding "true fulfillment by extending into eternity."[16] Nothing short of infinity and eternity can express God's vision for humanity. As David Watson puts it, "The life of God never ends, and we are being drawn into that divine life."[17]

When John testified to his experience of Jesus, the incarnate Word, he said both "We have seen his glory," and that Jesus wants us to "be with me where I am, and to see my glory" (John 1:14; 17:24 NIV). That glory which was inherently his, he in some way wanted to share with us. It is the

13. Westcott, *Epistles of St. John*, 98.

14. Marshall, *Epistles of John*, 172.

15. Sweet, *I am a Follower*, 105.

16. Nellas, *Deification in Christ*, 42.

17. Watson, *Scripture and the Life*, 2.

glory that shone through his words and miracles, his sacrifice (John 17:1), and his resurrection. It is the glory that sent the disciples sprawling on the ground at his transfiguration.

Mandell Creighton once said, "To me the one supreme object of human life is and always has been to grow nearer to God."[18] Spiritual growth is often seen as a part of the church's ministry, when in fact it is the point of ministry. Growing "nearer to God" is our ultimate destiny, but it also transforms the road we walk and those we encounter along the way. It is the remedy for "the unnatural situation in which man finds himself since the fall."[19] As Thomas Oden notes, "The new heavens and the new earth are a complete reversal of the whole history of sin. After the general resurrection and final judgment, a new beginning is made, which corresponds with the new creation of the resurrected life of Christian believers."[20] This reversal is what we delight to see and experience as it begins and progresses here and now. Just as we rejoice in each new milestone in a child's life, God rejoices in each step we take toward Christian maturity.

Recently there has been a "renewed interest" in what for too many of us is "a neglected doctrine."[21] Many Wesleyans have forgotten or downplayed the Wesleys' strong emphasis on Christian perfection. A.M. Allchin found "participation in God" to be "a forgotten strand in Anglican tradition."[22] Brian Daley acknowledges that "For most Catholics, it [the Feast of the Transfiguration] attracts relatively little attention compared with the other major liturgical events of the year."[23] Hans Boersma speaks of the reluctance of moderns to deal with heaven: "Evangelicals and Catholics alike have become more focused on the here-and-now than on the 'there-and-then.'"[24] Lutheran scholars, especially in Finland, have taken a fresh look at Martin Luther's theology to find at its core not a "forensic" salvation that leaves humanity unchanged, but the transforming presence of Christ, "the bridge to the Orthodox idea of salvation as deification or *theosis*."[25] Some Reformed theologians, from Calvin through Jonathan Edwards to T. F. Torrance, have

18. Creighton, in Rowell, "Michael Ramsey, Transfiguration," 201.

19. Nellas, *Deification in Christ*, 43.

20. Oden, *John Wesley's Teachings* 2:302.

21. Christensen and Wittung, *Partakers*, 11; Cf. Marshall, *Transfiguration of Jesus*, xi.

22. Allchin, *Participation*.

23. Daley, *Light on the Mountain*, 12.

24. Boersma, *Heavenly Participation*, 3.

25. Braaten & Jensen, *Union with Christ*, viii.

also seen the importance of *theosis*, while being very clear on what it is not. Myk Habets traces this heritage, even saying "The doctrine of theosis was not neglected in the Western tradition, not least within Reformed theology. It has been there all along, if underdeveloped."[26] In the words of T. F. Torrance,

> Let us become like Christ, since Christ became like us. Let us become divine for his sake, since he for ours became man. He assumed the worst that he might give us the better; he became poor that we through his poverty might be rich; he took the form of a servant that we might be exalted; he was tempted that we might conquer; he was dishonoured that he might glorify us; he ascended that he might draw us to himself, who were lying low in the fall of sin. Let us give all, offer all, to him who gave himself a ransom and reconciliation for us.[27]

The neglect or under-emphasis of the transfiguration in Western Christianity is radically out of sync with its theological and spiritual importance. That neglect obscures our vision of God and of our own place in the drama of salvation. As Dorothy Lee says, "The transfiguration story, with its wealth of symbolism, has something vital to say about divine glory and human transformation." It holds for us "a profound message of hope."[28] That hope both makes sense out of life and gives us reliable direction and motivating purpose. Too many Western Christians have lived with a truncated sense of the full reality of Christian hope.

The transfiguration and its implications for our destiny in Christ have long been at the forefront, however, of Eastern Orthodox theology and spirituality. In fact, it has often been in dialogue with Orthodox scholars that other traditions have seriously engaged this theology of transformation. But as Gosta Hallensten has said, "*Theosis*, deification, or divinization is no longer a topic limited to Eastern Orthodox thought. It is found almost everywhere."[29] Dorothy Lee notes that "Western Christianity in many places is struggling for survival against a deadly secularism that smothers any sense of transcendence or mystery," and that "The Church needs to regain

---

26. Habets, "Reforming Theosis," in Finlan and Kharlamov, *Theosis*, 151.

27. Torrance, in Habets, "Reforming Theosis," Finlan and Kharlamov, *Theosis*, 163; Cf. Baker, *T. F. Torrance and Eastern Orthodoxy*.

28. Lee, *Transfiguration*, 122, 124.

29. Hallonsten, "*Theosis* in Recent Research," in Christensen and Wittung, *Partakers of the Divine Nature*, 281.

the vision of Christ on the mountain, the light in which we see light . . . as the only source of hope for the transfiguration of a disfigured world."[30] It is perhaps a combination of the spiritual decline of the West and an increase in ecumenical openness that opens the hearts and minds of Western Christians to the full meaning of the transfiguration.

The theology of transfiguration and sanctification inspiring our Christian traditions is central to the Gospels and pivotal in the life of Christ. The transfiguration gives focus to the whole of Jesus' ministry and points to the ultimate purpose of his coming. To be sure, the transfiguration prepares him for the suffering ahead, but also looks beyond that suffering to his own resurrection and the destiny of the church. The transforming power of grace is central also to New Testament theology generally, and to the early church. While this focus may be new to many Western Christians, it is as old as the faith itself. What is needed is "a theology which engages the whole of the Christian tradition, in its diversity and richness."[31]

Several terms require clarification because of the way they are used in various traditions and because they can raise difficulties outside particular traditions. These include Christian "perfection," "holiness," "sanctification," "transfiguration," "transformation" and especially *theosis* and its equivalents, "divinization" and "deification." Also important are the "kingdom of God" and "participation in the divine nature" (2 Pet 1:4). Each term aims at the same reality from a different vantage point and often speaks most clearly within a particular culture. "Because it is a change in nature motivated by the Holy Spirit, the manner in which transformation occurs will always have an element of mystery."[32] We are formed in our various Christian traditions to prefer one term or another, but, more importantly, we are formed by God to be transformed so that his purpose in our creation becomes our destiny in his new creation. Since I am focusing on the interconnected process and promise inherent in these terms, although there are nuances peculiar to each one, I will often use them interchangeably.

Among Wesleyans and others, "Christian perfection" can itself be used in different ways, especially when it comes to issues of timing and eschatology. Yet both point to the transformation in Christ that restores the divine image in people, understanding that this change may happen suddenly in one instance and gradually in another, even in the same person.

---

30. Lee, *Transfiguration*, 2.

31. Medley, "Participation," in Kharlamov, *Theosis*, 2:235.

32. Long, *Quest for Holiness*, 79.

Although claiming much about instantaneous sanctification, John Wesley also recognized the progressive nature of Spirit-generated transformation, so that even perfection itself yields to further perfection appropriate to a person's stage in life and eternity. Because the term "perfection" so easily creates misunderstanding, I generally prefer other widely accepted biblical terms, including "transformation," "transfiguration," and "sanctification." A further term used in many traditions is "participation in the divine nature," (2 Pet 1:4): "Made flesh for our sake, / That we might partake, / The nature divine, / And again in his image, his holiness shine."[33]

Grace is absolutely foundational to our transformation in Christ. As Paul Collins has observed, "Perfection [for John Wesley] is understood in terms of the process of sanctification and is a work of grace."[34] In fact, "Perfection for Wesley is the goal of all humans under the condition of grace."[35] The Wesleys' understanding of Christian perfection draws from a broad ecumenical tradition, a significant part of which is directly linked to early Christian writers. At other points it is mediated through various Anglican and Protestant sources. Henry Scougal (1650–78), whose *The Life of God in the Soul of Man* exerted a major influence on the Wesleyan movement, "presents the architecture of the metaphor of deification before a Protestant and Evangelical audience," a mission extended by the Wesleys.[36] Along with Jeremy Taylor's *Holy Living and Holy Dying*, William Law's *A Practical Treatise upon Christian Perfection* and *A Serious Call to a Devout and Holy Life* also provided a vision of life thoroughly transformed by grace (But see Robert Tuttle's *Mysticism in the Wesleyan Tradition* for Wesley's disillusionment with law and much Western mysticism). Even when Wesley was not consciously drawing from certain ecumenical strands, because of common biblical and patristic roots, those strands can yield fruitful comparisons.

The less commonly used terms, "glorification" and "glorifying grace," refer to the process of sanctification in and beyond the transition from this life to the next. In this sense it is the extension of sanctification, but not a different reality. For this reason, I will generally use "sanctification" to precede *and* include glorification. Also, "sanctification" is closely related to holiness, which has several meanings, most pertinently appropriating the character of God. Ken Heer describes sanctification as "the process

33. Wesley, *Hymns for the Nativity,* 23.

34. Collins, *Partaking in Divine Nature,* 157.

35. Colon-Emeric, *Wesley, Aquinas,* 7.

36. Collins, *Partaking in Divine Nature,* 157.

that results in the condition of holiness."[37] If holiness is the goal, however, that goal is only partially realized at any given point, thus ever receding from view and taking the form of stations or milestones on the journey of sanctification.

Perhaps the most easily misunderstood term, especially for Western Christians and particularly for Protestants, is the Greek word *theosis* and its English equivalents (deification, divinization), which are indispensable but also troublesome. Often translated "becoming God," they may unintentionally suggest a kind of idolatry in which a created being is somehow transformed into the uncreated God. Within Lutheran circles, the term "Christification" has sometimes been used to get around this problem.[38] *Theosis* is commonly used in Orthodox theology and spirituality, yet even there we find careful explanations and clarifications of its precise intent. Chapter 6 will explore both the reality and meaning of *theosis*, including what it does *not* mean.

Because the confusion that necessitates disclaimers is likely to remain with words like "perfection" and "theosis," "divinization," or "deification," I will generally use "sanctification," "transformation," and "transfiguration" to include or express them, since these are New Testament terms that speak to a broad spectrum of Christians. In doing so, however, I do not in any way impugn the orthodoxy or accuracy of other terms. I will, of course, use *theosis* and its equivalents where appropriate in discussing Orthodox writings and others where they appear. While some may see terms like "transformation" and "sanctification" as inadequate to express the full reality of *theosis*, I believe these terms do communicate both the path and destiny by which God is restoring his creation in humanity and in the universe.

Bringing together the concepts of *theosis*, transfiguration, and sanctification is warranted by their common source in early Church writings and their common vision for grace-empowered transformation. Michael Christensen says,

> In my judgment, what Wesley taught as Christian perfection, holiness, or entire sanctification is both historically and theologically *derivative* and *dependent* on the more ancient doctrines of

37. Heer, *Ancient Fire*, 214.

38. For a similar use of "christification," in Thomas Aquinas, see Colon-Emeric, *Wesley, Aquinas, and Christian Perfection*, 8.

deification as taught by theologians in the Greek patristic tradition of the first four centuries."[39]

The English words "transformation" and "transfiguration" translate the same Greek word for "metamorphosis." While "transformation" may have a more general application, both words point in the same direction. Because of their similarity to "sanctification" and their essential place in the New Testament, I will use "transformation" and "transfiguration" in much the same way as "sanctification" throughout.

The essential reality of transfiguration and hope is a gift to all Christians. We have understood and expressed that reality in different ways, appropriate to the times, cultures, and traditions in which we have lived out our discipleship. Likewise there are and have been different ways of walking in and pursuing that reality. "There is and can be no single system, programme or sequence of growth applicable to all of us."[40] Two examples among very many are John Wesley's *Class Meetings* and Anthony Coniaris's Orthodox *Tools for Theosis*. Even "though there is no general prescription for life in God, there are certain basic conditions which we might keep in mind if we would make our way intelligently and not be victims of ignorance of the road to salvation."[41] Those "basic conditions" form the focus for this book. Each of us—within our own traditions, yet benefiting from parallels within the Great Tradition—must seek the grace-empowered sequence of growth that will take us reliably along that road.

The hope that is embodied in transfiguration begins in this life and extends infinitely beyond it. That hope is often associated with light, the light that is God (1 John 1:5) and the light of Christ in which we can walk (John 8:12; 1 John 1:7). First Peter 2:9 says that God has "called you out of darkness into his wonderful light" (NIV). While often this light is spiritual and figurative—referring to truth, goodness, and faithful discipleship— there were also times when it was *both* spiritual and visible, and of these the most memorable are the transfiguration and the conversion of Paul. Light also describes the new heaven and new earth, where "there will be no more night," for light from God will make lamplight and sunlight unnecessary

---

39. Christensen, "John Wesley," in Christensen & Whittung, eds., *Partakers*, 223, italics his; Cf. Outler, "John Wesley's Interests," in Oden and Longden, *Wesleyan Theological Heritage*, 97–110; Bence, "John Wesley's Teleological Hermeneutic"; Kimbrough, *Partakers of the Life Divine*; Tyson, *Charles Wesley on Sanctification*.

40. Sakharov, *We Shall See Him*, 85.

41. Sakharov, *We Shall See Him*, 85.

(Rev 22:5 NIV). The transfigured Christ of the transfiguration is also the everlasting Christ, and we are promised that he "will transform our lowly bodies so that they will be like his glorious body" (Phil 3:21 NIV).

All of this holds out the promise that we can, as Christ's ambassadors, "shine like stars in the universe," in a spiritual, yet figurative, sense right now, and that we "will shine like the sun in the kingdom of [our] Father" in a sense we can only imagine (Phil 2:15 NIV; Matt 13:43 NIV). All of this reflects Paul's astonishing prayer in Ephesians that through "love that surpasses knowledge" we may be "filled to the measure of all the fullness of God" (Eph 3:19 NIV). All this is possible because while we "were once darkness," he has made us "light in the Lord" (Eph 5:8 NIV). This, together with all the other glimpses of eternity in Scripture and the experience of the church, gives us hope that is eternal, that looks far beyond the confines and apparent futility of our temporary earthly existence. "Longing after the celestial world . . . is our delight and fills even sickly old age with the splendid hope of the Father's merciful embrace [Cf. Luke 15:20]."[42] In continuity with other Christian traditions and the New Testament itself, Coptic theologian Matthew the Poor "uses the story of the transfiguration . . . as a guiding metaphor for this divine transaction," the exchange by which Christ "became the Son of Man so that we might become sons of God in him, and he became human so that we might become deified in him."[43] Just as the transfiguration event in the Synoptic Gospels reveals something of the depth of Jesus' identity, likewise it reveals something of our own destiny in him, making that event and image the great symbol of our transformation in Christ.

With the apostle Paul, John and Charles Wesley, and others, the Eastern traditions have known that "the whole creation, and not only our bodies, is invited to this transfiguration."[44] The new creation is manifested both in individual believers and in universal transformation that restores the created order to God's original intent. This transformation is never a human achievement, but the work of grace. "Grace is not simply God's 'favor,' as wonderful as that is. Grace, in the end, is a participation in the life of God."[45] As Thomas à Kempis wrote:

42. Sakharov, *We Shall See Him*, 120–21.

43. Matthew the Poor, in Davis, *Coptic Christology in Practice*, 274.

44. Matthew the Poor, in Davis, *Coptic Christology in Practice*, 274.

45. Andrew D. Swafford, in Hofer, *Divinization*, 32.

Grace is a supernatural light and a special gift of God, the dis-
tinguishing mark of his chosen ones. It is an assurance of eternal
salvation. It raises a person from earthly things to the love of heavenly things, and it transforms him from a conceited, self-centered
person into a spiritual one."[46]

As Elmer Parsons notes, "God's saving grace, administered by the
Holy Spirit, enlightens us, calls us, entices us, empowers us, cleanses us
and helps us to become what God has always planned for us to be: his holy,
loving and beloved children (Eph. 1:4; 5:1–2)."[47]

In the accounts of Jesus' baptism in the Jordan, the Holy Spirit appears
"descending like a dove and alighting on him" (Matt 3:16 NIV); "descending
on him like a dove" (Mark 1:10 NIV); "in bodily form like a dove" (Luke
3:22). In the transfiguration passages, it could be said that the Holy Spirit
appears as the light radiating *from* Jesus to all who are gathered on the holy
mountain. Then, by grace, those who follow and are filled with "the light
of the world" (John 8:12 NIV) themselves become "the light of the world"
(Matt 5:14 NIV) as God's transforming power extends deep within each
person and radiates outward to the farthest reaches of the world. Summarizing Thomas Aquinas on divinization, Andrew Hofer says "our Christian life in grace bears the image of Christ himself. In this transformation
worked by grace, we become images of the One who is the perfect image
of God."[48]

I have not altered personal pronouns used by various, often historical
authors in reference to God or to human beings. Their words are quoted
as they were originally written or translated. In this way we avoid anach-
ronisms and honor the actual contributions of each writer. Thus, in some
cases, pronouns referring to God are capitalized, while others are in lower
case. Any apparent inconsistencies remain so that the integrity of each example is preserved. I have also preserved archaic spellings and expressions
as they appear in the sources. Scripture quotes are, unless otherwise indi-
cated, from the New International Version (2011). When quotes from the
Bible are used by quoted authors, they are in whatever translation each author chose to use (some of them carry no acknowledgment in the original).

Throughout this study, the theology and vision of the Wesleys is
supported by a wide variety of ecumenical sources, as well as those in the

46. à Kempis, *Imitation of Christ*, 152.
47. Parsons, "Experience of Sanctifying Grace," 871.
48. Hofer, *Divinization*, 69.

Introduction

Wesleyan tradition. Especially prominent are parallel and tributary references from Oriental and Eastern Orthodox writers. Thomas Hopko noted that "Methodists and Orthodox have been moved in recent years to return to the sources of their respective traditions." In exploring this common search (shared also by other Christian traditions), Hopko concludes, "what informed, instructed, and inspired the Orthodox church fathers and their disciples and John and Charles Wesley and their companions was exactly the same."[49]

49. Thomas Hopko, in Kimbrough, *Orthodox and Wesleyan Spirituality*, 7; 8, 9.

# Chapter 1

# God's Purpose and Human Destiny: "Too Heavenly Minded?"

May God himself, the God of peace, sanctify you through and through. May your whole spirit, soul and body be kept blameless at the coming of our Lord Jesus Christ. The one who calls you is faithful, and he will do it.

—1 Thess 5:23–24 NIV

Following the luminous Christ, we hope to fulfill our future in the transfiguring light of God.

—Andreas Andreopoulos, *Beloved Son*

Lord, what am I becoming? I know I'm becoming older, but am I becoming wiser, more loving, more forgiving, more gracious, more understanding, in a word, more like You? More God-like?

Am I striving to become by grace what you created me to be, or am I denying and covering over Your restored image in me through selfishness and greed?

Help me to aspire to the highest and the best and to use the power you offer me to become truly Your child as I partake more and more of Your love. Amen.

—Anthony Coniaris, *Achieving Your Potential*

You are to be a free and true person, going on to the destiny and freedom of the sons and daughters of God. Such people stand above present things and look toward eternal ones.

—Thomas à Kempis, *The Imitation of Christ*

Only a heavenly minded Christian faith will do us any earthly good.

—Hans Boersma, *Heavenly Participation*

IT WOULD BE DIFFICULT to overstate the distance between our own time and the nineteenth century, especially when it comes to attitudes about death and resurrection, heaven and hell, and the importance of dying well. However, there is a common expression that conveys a nearly complete misunderstanding of that earlier period, the saying that someone is "so heavenly minded they're no earthly good."

While this expression may fit some Christians and groups, it fails to represent the reality of Christianity in that century of amazing accomplishments. For Evangelicals and others, the nineteenth century was a time for building churches, colleges, and hospitals. There was a deep conviction that Christian faith could shape society and overcome social ills. Methodists and other Evangelicals believed they could accomplish anything by the power of God's Spirit. Motivated by a very activist faith, they shared the optimism of their time.

People were indeed heavenly minded, but far from distracting them from practical concerns, their vision of heaven propelled them into movements designed to do a great deal of earthly good. Timothy Smith's classic, *Revivalism and Social Reform*, documents the way this worked for Evangelicals before the Civil War. Among those who exemplify the connection between faith and action was James Finley, the Ohio circuit rider who devoted much of his energy to prison reform and to justice for Wyandot Indians.[1] The same spiritually fed activism typifies other groups of that time.

Later, as Evangelicalism in particular divided into Fundamentalist and Modernist camps, the connection weakened as those who emphasized "the old-time religion" grew pessimistic about the possibilities for change and devoted themselves to an increasingly disconnected, otherworldly spirituality.[2] Other traditions have their own histories of social involvement, of making a difference in this world while journeying beyond it.

The Coptic Orthodox monk Matthew the Poor once made a powerful connection between God's work within us and our participation in the world—our moral transformation: "What is left for us to do is to set the Holy Spirit free to work within us by opening up new possibilities in our behavior and actions—offering love to everyone, especially our enemies who curse us, abuse us, persecute us and plunder our property."[3] Given the long

---

1. Cole, *Lion of the Forest*.

2. Marsden, *Fundamentalism and American Culture*.

3. Matthew the Poor, *Titles of Christ*, 125; for a detailed study of transformation in the Coptic tradition, see Stephen Davis, *Coptic Christology in Practice*.

perseverance of Coptic Christianity in a precarious and often dangerous social context, he could hardly have made a stronger statement.

John Wesley's ministry offers a further example of spiritual religion "renew[ing] the face of the earth" (Ps 104:30 NIV). His mandate for the early Methodist preachers "to reform the continent, and spread scripture-holiness over these lands," was taken seriously by his movement, on both sides of the Atlantic.[4] Among those Wesley applauded and encouraged was William Wilberforce, whose tireless work eventually brought an end to the British slave trade.

Anyone who experiences genuine transfiguration will not leave the world unchanged. His or her participation in the world becomes different because it flows from what Leslie Weatherhead called "the transforming friendship."[5]

As Matthew the Poor wrote, "A person who is transformed in Jesus Christ is converted to the love, life, and light of God. And it is by the conversion of individuals that the world itself is transformed."[6] When we fail to provide each other with the vision of God's heavenly kingdom, we deprive ourselves of the inspiration and destination required for Christian discipleship. Lacking both the fuel and the hope to serve, we lose clarity as to our identity and purpose, and thus limited, we become little more than a mirror to the society around us. The message and experience of transfiguration restores meaning and direction for our lives, molding us and empowering us for today's work and for our ultimate destiny. The transforming connection with God offers a place to stand, a vantage point from which to evaluate and act upon the powerful currents of our own culture.

Could it be that today we are so earthly minded we don't think *enough* about heaven? While there remains a fascination that surfaces with books and films about near-death experiences and visions of heaven, Western churches are focused almost exclusively on this life and this world. There has been a relentless growth of secularism and materialism across our culture, but there is more. No doubt our turning away from thought about heaven is also a reaction against a shallow, self-centered, transactional view of salvation. There's something wrong with viewing heaven as merely an exchange for accepting Christ, a reward for good behavior (someone has

---

4. Coke and Asbury, *Doctrines and Discipline*, iii; Knight, "To Spread Scripture Holiness"; Cf. Dunning, *Reflecting the Divine Image*.

5. Weatherhead, *Transforming Friendship*.

6. Matthew the Poor, *Titles of Christ*, 154.

called it a "get out of hell free" card) or the endless continuation of life as we know it here, for example. In this context, Wesley's words ring loud and clear:

> By salvation I mean, not barely (according to the vulgar notion) deliverance from hell, or going to heaven, but a present deliverance from sin, a restoration of the soul to its primitive health, its original purity; a recovery of the divine nature; the renewal of our souls after the image of God in righteousness and holiness, in justice, mercy, and truth.[7]

Turning away from heaven, or viewing it mythologically, or in ways that are crudely self-serving has created a devaluing of older people, even as medical science extends longevity. Too often people who reach a certain age in our society are regarded as less important, not to be taken seriously. After all, how much do aging people have to contribute to a world that seems to leave them behind? How much do they have to hope for when most of the milestones valued by our society have come and gone? How do they fit in a culture of youth? What can the future hold when that future is temporary and superficial and hope operates within strict limitations? It is no wonder that people and organizations concerned with our aging population are seeking ways to make old age and retirement more meaningful, as well as more healthy.

Thomas à Kempis said it well in *The Imitation of Christ*: "It is vanity to wish for a long life and to care little about a good life. It is vanity to focus only on your present life and not to look ahead to your future life. It is vanity to live for the joys of the moment and not to seek eagerly for the lasting joys that await you." Indeed, "All that passes away with time is of little importance, and it passes away quickly."[8] Thus we read in the First Letter of John, "The world and its desires pass away, but whoever does the will of God lives forever" (1 John 2:17 NIV).

In a parallel reflection, Archimandrite George, abbot of one of the monasteries on Mount Athos, says:

> The question of the destiny of our lives is very serious, as it concerns the most important question for man: for what purpose are we placed on earth? If a man takes a correct stance on this issue; if he finds his true destiny; then he will be able to take a correct viewpoint in relation to particular questions that arise in daily life; in

---

7. John Wesley, *Farther Appeal*, Part I, in Cragg, *Works of John Wesley*, 11:106.

8. à Kempis, *Imitation of Christ*, 27; 135.

our studies, profession, marriage and the bearing and upbringing of children. If he does not relate correctly to this basic issue, then he will also fail in life's particular purposes, for what meaning can a particular purpose have if human life as a whole has no meaning?[9]

Attitudes about aging and the experience of aging will make only limited gains if we assume that this life sets an absolute limit to our hopes. The biological curve eventually tends downward, even if the curve gets longer. Those who believe or assume there is no life after death have little choice but to make this life as full and purposeful as possible, for as long as possible. Certainly this will improve the experience of old age, as far as it goes, but as far as it goes is not far enough. I agree with Gordon Rupp, who said, "We Christians have to be both this-worldly and other-worldly, or, rather, both-worldly."[10] For as Coptic Pope Senouda III put it, "deep inside every man is a nostalgia for eternity, and everything in the world is finite."[11]

Alexander Schmemann puts the issue starkly before us. A hopeless, earthbound world must see death

> not only as the end of life, but life itself as a senseless waste, as diminution and disappearance, life itself as a dying, already from the moment of birth; the transformation of the world into a cosmic cemetery; the hopeless subjection of man to disintegration, to time, and to death."[12]

Schmemann dismisses attempts to normalize death, saying that in fact death is our enemy, unnatural, to be conquered, and should neither be accepted nor adjusted to.[13] "Christianity is not reconciliation with death," says Schmemann. Instead, death is "the enemy to be destroyed," finally "'swallowed up in victory'" in Christ's resurrection.[14] By contrast, Nikolaos Vassiliadis says of the kingdom of heaven that "Whatever takes place there will not be 'an unhappy business' and 'vanity' (Eccl. 1:13; 2), filled with trouble, pain and tears. Life there will not be disturbance, anxiety or tragedy. . . . We will be journeying in worlds that are always new, unimaginably beautiful!"[15]

---

9. George, *Theosis*, 19.

10. Rupp, *Last Things First*, 79.

11. Shenouda III, *Characteristics of the Spiritual Path*, 15.

12. Schmemann, *O Death*, 82.

13. Ibid., 93, 94; 99, 100.

14. Ibid., 99 and 100; 1 Cor 15:26, 54 NIV.

15. Vassiliadis, *Mystery of Death*, 543, 544.

Gordon Rupp makes it very clear that this hope must be for individuals, not just vague collectives, as if some kind of survival without persons could even matter:

> Paul says that if Christ be not risen, our faith is vain. But we must also say that, if there is no individual survival, the resurrection of Christ becomes meaningless, and with it the life and death of Jesus of Nazareth. But the heart of the Christian hope is surely the belief that the love of Jesus for his friends could not be shattered by death, that it triumphed over the grave. And we have this hope for all who sleep in Christ, because if communion with God on earth is such that it can be called eternal life, how can we conceive of a God who would bring this to an end?[16]

The Christian message also has much to say about this life. While some would say it is *mainly* concerned with this life, Christianity paints a much fuller picture. For Christians, life is more than biology. Christian life mirrors the life of God. Hope extends far beyond the biological curve. In fact, there are no necessary limits to our future, because our future looks to the infinite, eternal nature of the One who is leading us forward on "the path of life."[17] As 1 John 2:17 notes, "The world and its desires pass away, but whoever does the will of God lives forever" (NIV). Again from Thomas à Kempis:

> This world is not your permanent home; wherever you may be you are a stranger, a pilgrim passing through. . . . Your place is in heaven, and you should see everything else in terms of heaven. All things pass away, and you pass away with them, too. See that you do not cling to passing things, lest you become caught up with them and perish along with them.[18]

Similarly, Coptic Orthodox bishop Youannis noted: "Heaven, as an idea, is not unusual to man—even if he does not express it with his own tongue—for it is deeply rooted within him and constantly attracts him."[19] Columbanus (c. 543–615), the Irish missionary monk, offers a similar reflection in one of his sermons:

---

16. Rupp, *Last Things First*, 74.

17. Ps 16:11 NIV; See Clarke, *Christian Theology*, 376–80.

18. à Kempis, *Imitation of Christ*, 65.

19. Youannis, *Heaven*, Ch. 1, n.p..

> And so, since we are travelers and pilgrims in this world, let us
> think upon the end of the road, that is of our life, for the end of
> our way is our home. . . . Many lose their true home because they
> have greater love for the road that leads them there. Let us not love
> the road rather than our home, in case we should lose our eternal
> home.[20]

When life is limited, in our minds at least, to the biological curve,
our purpose and goals are limited. Without the perspective of eternity, our
hopes must be restricted, and without the God of eternity, they may be
restricted to our own selfish desires or the shallow ambitions offered by our
own culture. Again from 1 John, "Everything that belongs to the world—
what the sinful self desires, what people see and want, and everything in
this world that people are so proud of—none of this comes from the Father; it all comes from the world" (1 John 2:16, TEV). John is justifiably
hard on human desires and ambitions, but there are other Scriptures that
acknowledge the value of ordinary, temporary human goals and values, as
long as they are secondary to the overarching reality of God's kingdom (for
example, Eccl 3:11–14, Matt 6:33).

It is true that there are people with an idealistic vision that is limited
to this life and lacking an explicit, motivating connection with God. I think
of the '60s protest singer Phil Ochs who, in his song "When I'm Gone," sang
about the urgency of altruistic goals he would not be able to accomplish
after death. I believe God inspired a portion of that vision and the singer's
desire to make a difference, even if the origin was not acknowledged. Sadly,
Ochs's vision lacked the clarity and depth of an eternal perspective, and
could not sustain him through experiences of depression and futility. His
life ended in suicide.

The tragic result of being so *earthly* minded we're no *heavenly* good
is that too many people are starved for hope. Without lifting their eyes to
eternity, their hopes dwindle and shrivel with each passing year. When
circumstances change or tragedy strikes, the appearance of diminishing
resources undermines resiliency and perseverance. People who have found
their identity in their work may retire to a life that seems empty and pur-
poseless, while people whose identity is in the everlasting, unchanging God
have a purpose greater than its expression in a career. There may be some
grinding of gears as they adjust to retirement, but the next gear propels
them into what is only a new chapter in living out their calling. Even if a

20. Columbanus, in Davies and O'Loughlin, *Celtic Spirituality*, 356.

society undervalues older people, their actual and ultimate value is derived from their connection with God, rather than their usefulness to an organization or the affirmation of others or the need to earn a living.

The problem, however, affects more than older people and retirees. We easily underestimate the importance of long-term hope for young and middle-aged adults. Life for everyone requires something worthwhile to look forward to, so any limit to that looking forward diminishes a person's life. Younger and middle-aged adults find their sense of purpose in many things, often including their children. Parents enjoy, encourage, and celebrate most of their children's advancing hopes as they grow up, but of course there comes a time when that relationship will change, and an empty nest may be for them what retirement is for people who have poured themselves into their work.

The great need is for a purpose that runs deeper and lasts longer than any other involvement, one that is solidly rooted in God. Only then can we give ourselves without losing ourselves, whether to family, work, or any other relationship or commitment. We can give ourselves without fear, knowing that every stage in life—even death itself—is finally a doorway to another stage, and every stage, whatever its challenges, is filled with its own particular blessings that we could only dimly imagine beforehand. Yet we confidently expect them, because we know the One who gives them and will always give them.

The church is, or should be, the greatest messenger of hope, but we fail to offer hope if we forget how much it matters! Not only do we fail the world, which desperately needs a word of hope, we also fail ourselves within the body of Christ. We can only change this by turning to our own message and mission. There is no lack of hope in Scripture! There is no lack of hope in Christian teaching! There is no lack of hope in the God we worship! The lack is in us when we neglect eternity and transfiguration as we pursue more immediate ends. We need to "set our hearts on things above," no matter how busily, and justifiably, we "serve the present age, our calling to fulfill."[21]

Pastors, teachers, youth leaders, and camp counselors (among others) place a high priority on spiritual growth. In that sense, we are people of hope. We take seriously the joy and blessings of growing, all through our

21. Col 3:1 NIV; Charles Wesley, "A Charge to Keep I Have," *United Methodist Hymnal*, #413, v. 2.

lives. Many churches offer study and prayer groups for people of all ages. But to what end?

Like parents, we get excited as children learn new skills. We rejoice as they learn to speak and walk and read. We encourage their progress in schools, colleges, and seminaries. We celebrate milestones with gift Bibles and Confirmation and baccalaureate services. We hope they will keep growing all through their lives. We do it because growing, especially spiritual growing, is obviously a good thing. But where will it eventually lead?

My own personal mission statement is adapted from 2 Peter 3:18, and that is to "grow [and help others to grow] in the grace and knowledge of our Lord and Savior Jesus Christ. To him be glory both now and forever! Amen" (2 Pet 3:18 NIV). To me, this is the most important contribution I can make to my family, friends, church, and world. It orients my life and enables me to prioritize my involvements, so I can dive into some things and say no to others. The glory spoken of in 2 Peter belongs to Jesus "now and forever." He shares that glory with us, "now and forever." The "glimpses of glory" we experience here and now make us yearn for a time—or rather an eternity—when joy will be "freely given to us in abundance."[22] But do we clearly communicate the importance of this reality?

Why would the church put so much energy into spiritual growth unless that growth has a clear purpose and direction? We work with children and youth because there is a new destination right around the corner—the next stage in their lives. We encourage adults to keep growing because growth equips them for their discipleship. But those limited reasons begin to wear thin as people age. What is our purpose in helping *older* adults to grow?

A partial answer is that it equips them for their discipleship at this particular time in their lives—perhaps encouraging and preparing them to mentor younger Christians, to model a positive vision for retirement, or demonstrate a transfigured life. It is also essential for each person, regardless of age, to continue growing, for our own sakes. Thomas Ryan rightly says, "People do not grow old, they are old when they stop growing." Retirement and old age offer "the opportunity to grow in new ways," and to discover new ways of living out our identity and purpose.[23] There are possibilities for solitude and focusing on things that matter. But what about the more distant future?

22. Adam, *Glimpses of Glory*; Habib, *Orthodox Afterlife*, 178.

23. Ryan, *Remember to Live!*, 23; 12.

I have often asked classes and retreat groups what they hope life will be like for them in five years. Most have little trouble with that one. Then I stretch the time to ten years, and twenty. This is more difficult, but after some reflection, there are usually some good responses. Then I move the time to 100 years, and they're stumped. Some think I'm joking. But after I explain the reason for my question, they're off and running.

A critical comparison juxtaposes the biological trajectory experienced by anyone who lives long enough, with the trajectory of divine transformation. The biological timeline resembles a bell-shaped curve, though we all know life doesn't go as smoothly as that. The first half of life, barring debilitating illness or injury or premature death, is one of upward movement filled with firsts. Facebook teems with news and photos of first steps and first words, the first day of kindergarten (and often of each grade thereafter), the first bicycle ride, the first year in t-ball, and the critical ability to read and write. There will be sports and travel, a first date, a prom, a driver's license, graduation from high school, and more. The adventures continue, through college and another graduation, perhaps the military, and sooner or later, a first job. Often there is marriage and the first child, perhaps with more to come. There will be a first house or apartment, a new career, new roles in the community. Then, sooner than anyone thought possible, someone throws an "over the hill" party—at least that's how it worked for me! There are jokes and "timely" gifts related to dentures and thinning hair. It is all in fun, but clearly there is something more serious going on, which is why some will experience midlife crises, or at least midcourse corrections, around this time.

Before long we may notice things we can no longer do as well as we once did. As years roll on, it may be harder to do the same work we once took in stride. Retirement may be on the horizon, if resources allow, and there may be illnesses to contend with. All of this may be accompanied by aging parents, who, for better or worse, remind us what's down the road. And on it goes. Few people get very excited about envisioning the end of the line.

As a child, I once had a terrifying dream of life as a gigantic wheel, on which everyone had a place. Each person, according to age, was moving along the surface of the wheel, which was itself moving. Young people were climbing and moving forward as their side of the wheel moved toward the top. Those in the prime of life were at or near the top, "on top of the world," but only for a moment. Soon the relentlessly moving wheel was rushing those same adults down the other side, toward the bottom. As they moved closer and closer to the ground, they grew increasingly desperate. Some made futile attempts to turn around and regain the top, but the natural upward movement that aided them when they were younger had become a natural downward movement, hastening their demise. Soon they would be crushed by the same wheel they rode to the top. I woke up horrified, grasping even then that nothing in (and confined to) this life could dispute its reality.

All of this is just a sampling of what may appear on the world's biologically based trajectory. Its promises are limited, and its last end is death. But the trajectory of spiritual transformation looks very different. All the same bell-shaped possibilities apply, but there is much more to the picture, like an overlay. That "much more" has dimensions of depth, meaning, and the Spirit that give life to everything we do. This trajectory is marked and driven by the panorama of grace that grows more powerful in us as we repeatedly or continually open ourselves to receive it. The grace is always at God's initiative and always requires our cooperation. Grace is reliable, abundant, and available. Its purpose is to connect our lives more and more with the life of God in a transformation that restores God's image in us, the image in which humanity was originally created. This trajectory of the Spirit even conquers our "last enemy," death itself, for in the words of the ancient Easter hymn and proclamation, "Christ is risen from the dead, trampling down death by death, and upon those in the tombs bestowing life."[24]

This trajectory is not at all like a bell-shaped curve, but is more like a straight line, beginning early in life and moving onward and upward toward a future that is infinite and eternal, just as God is infinite and eternal. Like the biological trajectory, this one is not as smooth as it appears from a distance, but its direction is sure, as long as it rests on the synergy of God's grace and our willing cooperation. Once we embark on this journey, "What has been begun in us is intended to progress and grow, in order to reach its completion in the life of heaven."[25] That "completion" never reaches an end, because it reflects the endlessness of God.[26] Our growth in grace, even after death, is "an eternal progress into the inexhaustible riches of the divine

24. First Corinthians 15:26 NIV; Alfeyev, *Christ the Conqueror of Death*.
25. Keating, *Deification and Grace*, 61.
26. Cf. Nellas, *Deification in Christ*, 51.

life."[27] At every stage, in this world and the next, progress in sanctification comes by grace:

> The initiative always lies with God. Human salvation was God's idea, accomplished by Christ as a free gift of grace. Our ability to respond to the gracious work of God is itself "graced." Grace always comes before and initiates every human response to the offer of salvation in Christ—it is "prevenient." Consequently, there is no room for human boasting: "What do you have that you did not receive? And if you received it, why do you boast as if it were not a gift?" (I Cor 4:7)[28]

Paul brings these two trajectories together in a way that puts all this in the perspective of eternity:

> Therefore we do not lose heart. Though outwardly we are wasting away, yet inwardly we are being renewed day by day. For our light and momentary troubles are achieving for us an eternal glory that far outweighs them all. So we fix our eyes not on what is seen, but on what is unseen, since what is seen is temporary, but what is unseen is eternal." (2 Cor 4:16–18 NIV)

That inward renewal and growth needs to happen all through our lives. Growth is essential to hope in this life, and even before old age requires us to progressively abandon certain earthly hopes, we need to grow in preparation for the new life that follows death. To give up on growing, or to see no point in growing, is to give up on life now and to enter eternity unprepared. A line from one of Bob Dylan's early songs serves well as a warning, "that he not busy being born is busy dying."[29] It does matter whether our lives fit into the grand scheme of things when that scheme is God's purpose for our lives and for the kingdom. Clarifying our purpose and our destiny, far from rendering us no earthly good, empowers us to focus our energies where they will do the most good, where our lives will not only be fruitful, but will grow eternally as God's image is more and more perfectly restored in us, by the power of the Spirit.

This kind of vision opens up an eternity worth living and longing for. "We shall see the Lord and we shall be filled by the greatest, the holiest and the purest delight; that brightest radiance, which shone upon the holy

27. John Meyendorff, in Allchin, *Participation in God*, 6; Cf. Clarke, *Christian Theology*, 377.

28. Keating, *Deification and Grace*, 67.

29. Dylan, "It's Alright, Ma I'm Only Bleeding."

Apostles at the most divine Transfiguration of Christ, will shine around us." This vision, focused in the transfiguration and spoken of in Jesus' teaching, has the capacity to draw us forward on the path of life and through the gates of heaven, for it is not only our own personal transfiguration, but "the transfiguration of the world."[30]

The vision of Christ and eternal glory embodied in the transfiguration is one to inspire hope beyond anything this world can offer, for "One day we will see Him as He is; the light of His countenance will be reflected on our faces, and we will be like Him."[31] It is a vision that lifts us beyond time, even as we live within time, to a dimension that transcends time and offers glimpses of eternity, for "it is the knowledge of God that saves man from falling under the dominion of time and its illusory finality in death." The transfiguring connection with God "inevitably causes us to rise above the passage of time and death till we sense that we are greater than time, higher than events, and truer and more lasting than death."[32]

A. M. Allchin points to "the intuition of Gregory of Nyssa, that eternal life is something which is open-ended, an infinite progress into a life which is by definition, infinite."[33] The journey begun in this life extends beyond limits into the next, offering us limitless hope for spiritual progress beyond our imagination, yet available as a mysterious gift (See 1 Cor 2:9–10). The human soul, designed for this eternity, "can still become . . . a window into life in heaven."[34] It can know and reveal something of the mystery of eternal, infinite life. Such a revelation is an extraordinary blessing in this world.

In *The Idea of Perfection*, R. Newton Flew concludes: "Christianity is impoverished unless it be preached as a Gospel of hope for this world as the next, as a Gospel that all things are possible to faith, because faith is set on a living God who has a purpose for us in this world and in the life beyond."[35] As David Adam says of the present/future promise of heaven:

> He came down with a purpose, to raise you up. He died that you
> might live and have lifei n all its fullness. He entered the grave that
> you might rise to the fullness of eternal life. He became human

---

30. Vassiliadis, *Mystery of Death*, 574.
31. Matthew the Poor, *Words for Our Time*, 92.
32. Matthew the Poor, *Communion of Love*, 42.
33. Allchin, *God's Presence Makes the World*, 59.
34. Matthew the Poor, *Orthodox Prayer Life*, 121.
35. Flew, *Idea of Perfection*, 415–16.

that you might share in the divine. This is not just for a future life, it is for now: lift up your heart and rejoice.[36]

It may be possible to distort Christian hope so that a person is so heavenly minded as to be no earthly good. But that is an unnecessary, and in our time rare, distortion, one that frustrates the working of grace in humanity. In fact, to be led by grace on a pilgrimage of eternal hope is to be in a position to make the highest possible contribution to this world.

36. Adam, *Encompassing God*, 20.

# Chapter 2

# What Actually Happened at the Transfiguration?

We were eyewitnesses of his majesty . . . when we were with him on the sacred mountain.

—2 Pet 1:16–18 NIV

As we gaze on your kingly brightness, so our faces display your likeness, ever changing from glory to glory, mirrored here may our lives tell your story.

—Graham Kendrick, "Shine, Jesus, Shine"

You were transfigured upon the mount, O Christ our God, revealing Your glory to Your disciples as much as they were able to bear. So that when they saw You crucified, they would know it voluntary, and would proclaim to the ends of the earth that You are the Light of the Father.

—*Kontakion of the Transfiguration, Orthodox Monastery of the Transfiguration*

The Lord of all is the treasure store of all things: upon each according to his capacity He bestows a glimpse of the beauty of his hiddenness, of the splendor of His majesty. He is the radiance who, in his love, makes everyone shine.

—Ephrem the Syrian, *Hymns on Paradise*

Through the Transfiguration of Christ our own end and purpose becomes visible.

—Andreas Andreopoulos, *Metamorphosis*

FOR TOO MANY OF US, the transfiguration story comes across as weird, exotic, and remote. We read it and wonder, shrug our shoulders and move on, unsure of its meaning, or its relevance for Christian faith and life. Because we tend to move on, many fail to fully appreciate this strange and wonderful moment in the Gospels. Dorothy Lee calls the transfiguration "one of the most neglected stories in the New Testament" among Western Christians.[1]

That neglect is not shared by Eastern Christians, who see that in the transfiguration, Jesus

> wanted to give his disciples a view of the kingdom of God, about which he had often talked to them, in anticipation of the difficult times that were waiting ahead. It was necessary to see the divine light of the Transfiguration at the end of the tunnel of the Crucifixion.[2]

In that moment on the holy mountain,

> what Christ chose to do was not to give to his disciples and to humanity only words and instructions, but to lift, even if briefly, the curtain that separates this world from the presence of God, and to give his disciples the experience of the kingdom.[3]

In other words, to match his earlier words of warning, he also gave them hope.

So what actually happened there on the sacred mountain? Irenaeus, one of the earliest Christians to write on the subject, saw the transfiguration story as "authentically accurate."[4] Brian Daley says "The word 'transfigured' is clearly meant to convey a complete change of appearance, at least."[5] While some may dismiss the transfiguration or explain it away, I agree with Andreas Andreopoulos: "We believe that this event was real and not symbolic, abstract, allegorical, or metaphysical."[6] As Gregory Palamas once said, "This light of Transfiguration was not a hallucination but will remain for eternity and has existed from the beginning."[7] Instead of demythologizing or ignoring it, I believe that Scripture, and the nature and mission of Christ, calls us to take the transfiguration seriously and to explore its implications

1. Lee, *Transfiguration*, 1.

2. Andreopoulos, *This Is My Beloved Son*, 86.

3. Andreopoulos, *This Is My Beloved Son*, 86.

4. McGuckin, *Tranfiguration of Christ in Scripture*, 101.

5. Daley, *Light on the Mountain*, 16.

6. Andreopoulos, *This Is My Beloved Son*, 18.

7. Andreopoulos, *Metamorphosis*, 224.

for our lives. For "the glory of the Lord is a paradigm of the glory that he will bestow upon all his faithful."[8] The hope this offers *us* is as critical and decisive as the hope offered to Jesus' disciples. Thus the transfiguration is "an emblem of humanity glorified at the resurrection."[9]

Acknowledging the skepticism of some New Testament scholars, Michael Ramsey asks,

> Was it an objective occurrence or a vision seen by one or all of the three disciples present? The answer will turn in part upon our belief concerning the person of Jesus Christ. If the view of His person which was held by the evangelists and the apostolic Church in general is true, then a frankly supernatural occurrence in the course of his earthly ministry will be credible.[10]

For R. Hollis Gause, "The Transfiguration account is designed to present a historical event in the life of Jesus; it is an event that presents the nature of the kingdom of God."[11] It is not a useful myth, but an actual event, one that radiates the power of its glory in transforming those who catch its vision. Pope Shenouda III says that "Jesus is seen on the Mount of Transfiguration . . . where humanity was mesmerized and awestruck. There *His face shone like the sun.* Even His clothes became as white as light (Matt 17:2). His amazing incredible brilliance was like a token of our existence after our own resurrection for we will become like Him" (italics his). In fact, "His transfiguration was the first-fruits of the transfiguration of human nature."[12]

Michael Ramsey places the transfiguration "at a watershed in the ministry of Jesus . . . a height from which the reader looks down on one side upon the Galilean ministry and on the other side upon the *Via Crucis* [Way of the Cross]."[13] That watershed reaches even farther back to the Old Testament and forward to the new creation, symbolized by the presence of Moses and Elijah. Much has been said about their presence acknowledging Jesus' ministry as the fulfillment of their own. In Luke's Gospel, Moses and Elijah speak with Jesus about his coming departure (literally "exodus"), "which he was about to bring to fulfillment at Jerusalem" (Luke 9:31 NIV).

8. McGuckin, *Transfiguration of Christ in Scripture,* 120.

9. Watson, *Biblical and Theological Dictionary,* 916.

10. Ramsey, *Glory of God,* 106.

11. Gause, "Lukan Transfiguration Account," 230.

12. Shenouda III, "Holy Transfiguration," 321; 5.

13. Ramsey, *Glory of God,* 101.

Rob Marshall sees this exodus signifying "deliverance as it had in the past," and like the past, coming at a price.[14] But the deliverance would accomplish our redemption, our transfiguration, which would more than justify that price, without trivializing it for a moment. The disciples would, in their own sometimes stumbling way, face Jerusalem with Jesus, but because of that journey, they could also "live with him" and even "be like him" (2 Cor 13:4; 1 John 3:2 NIV).

Jesus showed his disciples, including us, the destination of their journey with him. The disciples are given "a proleptic vision of his glory in the present," an immediate fulfillment of his promise that they would "see the Son of Man coming in his kingdom."[15] Douglas Moo notes that

> each [Synoptic] evangelist places just before the Transfiguration a prediction that some of his disciples would see "the kingdom of God" (Luke 19:27) / "the Son of man coming in his kingdom" (Matt. 16:28) / "the kingdom of God come with power" (Mark 9:1)—the fulfillment of which comes in the Transfiguration.[16]

The great Armenian theologian and poet Gregory of Narek wrote:

> As they witnessed the overwhelming sight of your splendid transfiguration, terrified by your light and divine radiance, they fell to the ground half dead.[17]

Through the mystery of his Transfiguration, Christ

> Revealed . . . on Mount Tabor to your holy apostles and prophets, the radiance of your Divinity to us transients, even after them.[18]

There would be strange and horrible days ahead, days of confusion and persecution, but those days would end in unimaginable glory. A process of grace was at work, beautifully described by Paul in 2 Corinthians 3:18: "And we all, who with unveiled faces contemplate the Lord's glory, are being transformed into his image with ever-increasing glory, which comes from the Lord, who is the Spirit" (NIV). Michael Ramsey calls the transfiguration "a disclosure, before the Passion, of the glory which was in store

---

14. Marshall, *Transfiguration of Jesus*, 87.

15. Keener, *Commentary on the Gospel of Matthew*, 436; Matthew 16:28 NIV.

16. Moo, *2 Peter, Jude*, 80.

17. Terian, *Festal Works of St. Gregory*, 134.

18. Terian, *Festal Works of St. Gregory*, 134.

for Christ and for the disciples."[19] As Andreas Andreopoulos points out, the Greek word behind "transfiguration" and "transformation" is the same. Impossible as it may sound, ours is a "transfiguration into the image and the glory of God."[20] There can be no greater hope!

Nor was this hope an impossible dream. Human nature, by itself, shrinks from such a vision, but the journey of transfiguration is made not by ourselves, but by the power of the Spirit.

> Within the limitations of our nature, we have no more hope of reaching God than a mad boatman in the night who hopes to row all the way to the moon that is reflected on the water. And yet, the miracle of the Transfiguration shows us that the grace of God covers the distance."[21]

We make this journey only with the help of Scripture and the wisdom and experience of those who have made it before us. The rules and guidelines they offer are not in themselves a path to achievement, but simply a description of the path on which God leads us. The power that enables us to travel is grace.[22] "Godliness is not the result of our own effort, but the gift of God's transforming grace."[23]

The transfiguration of Christ on the mountain was and remains a convergence between heaven and earth. In one sense, heaven is never far away, as in Psalm 139: "I can never escape from your Spirit! I can never get away from your presence" (Ps 139:7 NLT)! But heaven often seems very far away, and we need what Celtic Christians have called "thin places," where the distance is bridged. Thin places are those in which divine and human meet; where God's presence breaks or has broken through to his people in powerful, transformative ways. Jacob's Bethel, the Holy Land generally, and Christian pilgrimage destinations around the world can all be considered thin places.

As Andreopoulos has noted, "There is no other place in the entire Bible where the curtain between the material world and the invisible world is completely lifted visually, and there is no other place where the divinity of Christ is witnessed in such a dramatic way."[24] While the three disciples were

---

19. Ramsey, *Glory of God*, 34.

20. Andreopoulos, *This Is My Beloved Son*, 14.

21. Ibid., 129.

22. See Casey, *Guide to Living*, 57.

23. Barker et al., *Reflecting God*, note for Ephesians 4:24, 1798.

24. Andreopoulos, *Metamorphosis*, 41–42.

the first and most direct witnesses, we too see something of Jesus' glory as we enter into their story. As Nikolaos Vassiliadis says:

> A vague taste of that blessedness is ours when we remember the sacred emotions felt by the three Apostles, who were present at the holy Transfiguration of the Savior when He shone like the sun. As we know, at His holy Transfiguration, the Savior showed His disciples only a small portion of the light of His divinity; He revealed to them only some vague and limited features of His divine glory.[25]

Again, what exactly happened at the transfiguration? Gregory Palamas made it clear that

> Christ was transfigured not by receiving something he did not have before, nor by being changed into something he previously was not, but as manifesting to his disciples what he really was, opening their eyes and from blind men making them see again.[26]

What the disciples saw was

> the same divine nature Christ always had, although it was not possible to see it. The Transfiguration, then, stands in the middle of the tenure of Christ as the only moment when Christ is revealed as he really is during his earthly ministry and before the Second Coming.[27]

According to the Venerable Bede, "The disciples truly saw him coming into his kingdom when they saw him shining in glory on the mountain."[28] Joel B. Green makes the same point when he says, "As Jesus promised . . . these apostles have now seen, if only for a moment, the consummation of the kingdom, for they have seen the Son, the Chosen One, in his glory."[29]

The disciples who witnessed and took part in the transfiguration encountered Jesus in a way they had never experienced. There was no way they could understand what they saw and heard and felt, but eventually they could tell their story, and the Holy Spirit would unpack their experience. They participated in, as well as observed, "the glory of God in the face of Jesus Christ" (2 Cor 4:6 ESV), and as Matthew the Poor notes, "Simply

25. Vassiliadis, *Mystery of Death*, 552.
26. Gregory Palamas, in McGuckin, *Transfiguration of Christ in Scripture*, 113.
27. Andreopoulos, *Metamorphosis*, 224.
28. Bede, in McGuckin, *Transfiguration of Christ in Scripture*, 291.
29. Green, *Gospel of Luke*, 379.

by entering God's presence does a person receive glory!"[30] They also were seeing something of their own destiny, though without understanding it for a long time to come. Yet in this moment "Jesus not only shines with glory, but also transforms everything and everyone around him, bathing all with glory."[31] Bernie Owens rightly describes Peter, James, and John as "overwhelmed with awe and forced to their knees by the brilliant manifestation of his divine nature," but I believe he takes things too far when he says "they nevertheless knew in some sense that the same transformation and transfiguration process was to happen to them someday in God's providence."[32] Owens is right about the implications of their experience, but surely they could not have understood those implications yet, even in a preliminary way. At that moment, as R. Hollis Gause points out, these disciples reacted in understandable fear. From their immersion in stories of the Old Testament, they

> correctly understood this cloud to be the descent of the presence of God among them. This recognition is the reason for the fear of the disciples as they entered the cloud. This is the usual reaction of men in Scripture who come into the divine presence.[33]

Even so, as we read and imaginatively enter the story, we can begin to see and appreciate what was happening and what it meant and still means. We can benefit from Paul's astonishing words in 2 Corinthians 3:18: "And we all, who with unveiled faces contemplate the Lord's glory, are being transformed into his [Christ's] image with ever-increasing glory, which comes from the Lord, who is the Spirit" (NIV). We can at least begin to take in, though without anything like complete understanding, the idea that somehow we "may participate in the divine nature" (2 Pet 1:4 NIV). And we can perhaps begin, in amazement and humility, to reflect on John's promise "that when Christ appears, we shall be like him, for we shall see him as he is" (1 John 3:2 NIV).

One fascinating aspect of the transfiguration story is the appearance of Moses and Elijah with Christ on the mountain. Moses' prophecy of "a prophet like me" (Deut 18:15; Acts 3:22) is fulfilled in his presence, and Moses' warning, "You must listen to everything he tells you" (Acts 3:22), or

---

30. Matthew the Poor, *Words for Our Time*, 92.

31. Humphrey, *Grand Entrance*, 4, 46.

32. Owens, *More than You Could Ever Imagine*, 6.

33. Luke 9:34; Gause, "Lukan Transfiguration Account," 115.

the shorter "You must listen to him" (Deut 18:15) is echoed and completed in the Father's words, "This is my Son, whom I love. Listen to him" (Mark 9:7 NIV; Cf. Matt 17:5 and Luke 9:35). For the three disciples, these key figures from Israel's history must have in some sense pointed to the One who was now before them, the One to whom the entire Old Testament looked forward. Like Moses, Elijah had a decisive encounter with God on a mountain (1 Kgs 19:8–18). Now they both appear on the Mount of Transfiguration and in that appearance their lives and ministries are fulfilled.[34] Edith Humphrey sees that in this event "the people of God are gathered around Jesus: old covenant believers are represented by Moses and Elijah, and the new covenant Church by the three apostles."[35] Beyond that, for Pope Shenouda III, "Moses and Elijah in their transfiguration represent the whole human nature." At some length he shows how their presence on the mountain symbolizes the promised transfiguration of all kinds of people and all forms of discipleship.[36] On the mountain, Moses and Elijah represent not only their own roles as prophets, now completed and superseded by Jesus, but also the transformation which brought them into that moment and beyond as far more than ancient corpses or ghostly apparitions. They are part of the restored humanity of God's new creation.

R. H. Gause points out that

> The cloud which descends over the Transfiguration scene is the Shekinah. It is eschatological and it fulfills the kingdom concept by overshadowing . . . the entire company—Jesus, Moses and Elijah (all appearing in glory), and Peter, John and James. They are all incorporated into the kingdom.[37]

Though these disciples remained within the limitations of this world, they experienced at close range the direction and goal of their lives. They experience in advance the glory of the coming kingdom.[38]

The three disciples had experienced a view of the apocalyptic kingdom which they must preserve and cherish, but which could not continue as a way of life. It could not continue because the exodus at Jerusalem had not taken place.[39]

34. Andreopoulos, *This Is My Beloved Son*, 55–59.

35. Humphrey, *Grand Entrance*, 45.

36. Shenouda III, "Holy Transfiguration," 5; 6–8.

37. Gause, "Lukan Transfiguration Account," 233.

38. Ibid., 185; 151.

39. Ibid., 130.

The transfiguration epitomizes the traditional exchange formula: "The Son of God became man in order that men might become sons of God. He took what is ours, to give us what is his."[40] Bede said,

> When the Lord was transfigured before the disciples he revealed to them the glory of his own body which was to be manifested through the Resurrection. He shows how great will be the splendor of the future bodies of the elect after the Resurrection. On this matter he says elsewhere: "Thus shall the just shine like the sun in the Kingdom of their Father," and here as a sign of his own future splendor his face is as radiant as the sun.[41]

Thus the Christian hope is not a disembodied immortality, but a transformed, embodied person: "He will refashion the body of our lowliness then and make it conform to the body of his own glory."[42]

> So now I beseech you, reach out and lift up the eyes of your mind towards the light of the Gospel preaching so that you may be yourself transfigured in the renewal of your minds [Romans 12:2], attracting the divine rays from on high and becoming conformed to the likeness of the glory of the Lord whose face on the mountain shone today as radiant as the sun.[43]

Thus "we see ourselves conformed to the glory of his body in the Kingdom of the Father, shining with the splendor of the sun; that splendor through which he showed the apostles what his kingdom was like when he was transfigured on the mountain."[44] The disciples were the first to see this vision, to experience—though certainly not to understand—this fuller reality of Christ and at least a hint of their own destiny. "For all their misunderstanding, incoherence, confusion and fear, the three disciples on the mountain are given a vision of hope and joyful expectation," and that vision is now ours to share.[45] They are allowed a glimpse of Christ and, in a different way, themselves as "the light of the world" (John 8:12; Matt 5:14 NIV).

We receive all this in a spirit of wonder, knowing that God "is able to do immeasurably more than all we ask or imagine, according to the power

---

40. Arzoumanian, *Studies in Armenian Church*, 59.

41. Matthew 13:43; Bede, in McGuckin, *Transfiguration of Christ in Scripture*, 124–25.

42. Anastasios of Antioch, in McGuckin, *Transfiguration of Christ in Scripture*, 193.

43. Gregory Palamas, in McGuckin, *Transfiguration of Christ in Scripture*, 234.

44. Hilary of Poitiers, in McGuckin, *Transfiguration of Christ in Scripture*, 260.

45. Lee, *Transfiguration*, 124.

that is at work within us" (Eph 3:20 NIV). We pray in the spirit of one who asked the Lord to take away "the weaknesses of my flesh and increase in me the graces of your Holy Spirit that I may become a temple and dwelling place for your glory."[46]

For by grace Jesus "creates within us the capacity to live fully the life of God and, at the same time, to be the fullness of who we are, of all we are being created to be."[47] Who was transfigured on the holy mountain? As Andreas Andreopoulos notes,

> What changed was the way the three apostles saw their teacher. For the first time they could see his divinity, although he was always God, even when his divinity was hidden. The real change was not in the face or the clothes of Christ, but in the way Peter, John, and James became, by the power of the Holy Spirit, direct participants with the divinity of the Father that was shining to them through Christ.[48]

New Testament scholar Paul Hammer points out that there is a progression in Mark's account of incidents in which Jesus is proclaimed as the "Son of God." In the first (Mark 1:11 NIV), the voice from heaven speaks to Jesus himself at his baptism, saying "You are my Son, whom I love; with you I am well pleased." (In Matthew, even at the baptism, the voice says "This is," but Luke repeats Mark's rendition.) In the second proclamation (Mark 9:7 NIV), "a voice came from the cloud: 'This is my Son, whom I love. Listen to him.'" In this case, the Father's voice speaks directly to the disciples, and, through them, to us. Finally, with Jesus on the cross (Mark 15:39 NIV), it is a Roman soldier who says, "Surely this man was the Son of God!" This last case is an unexpected epiphany, as the gospel is shared even by a gentile centurion, a representative of the world for which Christ died.[49]

What happened at the transfiguration is the revelation in time and space of the mysterious light and glory of God in Christ, and with it the vision of human destiny in God's new creation. That revelation and that vision would empower Jesus' disciples for the terrible road ahead by giving them an unforgettable experience of the eternal kingdom.

---

46. Mathews, "First Glance," in Ervine, *Worship Traditions in Armenia*, 166.

47. Owens, *More than You Could Ever Imagine*, 7.

48. Andreopoulos, *This Is My Beloved Son*, 34.

49. Paul Hammer, interview with author, 1–8–2013; Cf. Witherington III, *Gospel of Mark*, 262.

# Chapter 3

# God with Us: Incarnation and Transfiguration

Christ in the incarnation caught up humanity to heaven.
—Daphne D. C. Pochin Mould, *Irish Pilgrimage*

Lord, we are able. Our spirits are thine. Remold them, make us, like thee, divine.
—"Are Ye Able," *The United Methodist Hymnal*

Made flesh for our sake,

That we might partake,

Thy nature divine,

And again in his image, his holiness shine.
—Charles Wesley, *Hymns for the Nativity*

If the Creator in all was made like unto man [Heb. 2:17], it follows that man was created with the possibility of being like unto God in all things: "We shall be like him, for we shall see him as he is" [1 John 3:2].
—Sophrony Sakharov, *We Shall See Him as He Is*

Emmanuel did not stop at fulfilling "God with us," but desired that we too should be with Him! This reveals to us the hidden secret in Emmanuel. God came to live with us for a definite purpose: that we ourselves should live with Him. For what would the point be of all the sacrifice and redemption which cost the Father the offering of His beloved Son to the sufferings of humiliation and death? Is it not for us to be with Him in the end?!
—Matthew the Poor, *The Titles of Christ*

THERE IS A CLEAR and purposeful line connecting the incarnation of Christ to his transfiguration, and on to the transformation of his people and the restoration of creation. The incarnation was God's decisive answer to the tragic drama of the human race. Death, grim and unrestrained, enters [with the fall] violently into the world to change radically our life; to deprive us of our blessed communion with God and to terminate our journey toward eternal and incorruptible life."[1] John of Damascus made explicit the link between incarnation and transfiguration when he spoke of Christ "becoming human in nature and form, so that the uncontainable God might be available to men and women revealing through himself and in himself the brilliance of the divine nature."[2] The new creation in each person and in the universe is the ultimate goal of everything Jesus said and did. The transfiguration itself is the paramount image of that new creation.

There is an evangelical cliché that Jesus was born to die. Like all clichés, there is a partial truth in this one. Jesus was not born for a life of comfort or political power, for example. He was not born merely to teach or to work miracles for their own sake. His death was freely accepted and inescapable—a built-in feature of the incarnation. But crucifixion was not his *ultimate* purpose or the final cause of his life and ministry.[3] The salvation he won is also more than a superficial transaction in which the cross pays for our sin and protects us from punishment. "'Our Lord Jesus Christ became man not only to save us from sin, but also to restore completely that communion with God, which we had lost. The Lord became man, so that 'we may become gods,' writes St. Athanasios the Great,"[4] Vassiliadis says. He then adds, "But what do we mean when we say 'deification of our human nature and divinization of the righteous?' We mean that human beings become through deification 'partakers of the divine nature' (II Pet. 1, 4), they become 'sons by participation,' by virtue of the Incarnation."[5]

The ultimate reason for Jesus' birth, death, and resurrection was and is the restoration of the image of God in us—our transfiguration—and through us, the restoration of the entire creation to its original wholeness.

1. Vassiliadis, *Mystery of Death*, 63.

2. John of Damascus, in Daley, *Light on the Mountain*, 210.

3. See Kallistos Ware in Keating, *Deification and Grace*, 25.

4. Vassiliadis, *Mystery of Death*, 545. See chapter 6 for needed clarification on language that comes across as audacious and troubling to Westerners.

5. Vassiliadis, *Mystery of Death* 546; See Daley, *Hope of the Early Church*, esp. 32 and 204, for the pattern of reflection on divinization within eschatological teaching, from Irenaeus to John of Damascus.

So we read in Matthew the Poor that by taking on our flesh and living our life, he "fills it with his divinity, and it receives 'from his fullness grace upon grace' (John 1:16)."[6] Irenaeus expresses this connection as Christ "raising man to God by his incarnation."[7]

Fr. Matthew makes the point very clearly: "To Christ redemption meant in the first place something beyond forgiveness and reconciliation—to restore the love and eternal life we had lost through transgression and separation from God." Here again he focuses on the divine purpose behind the incarnation, which is far more than a superficial rescue mission that leaves our human nature unchanged. Salvation or redemption is not merely a change in our legal status before God, but rather a process of transformation that restores in us the image of God. Thus Christ's purpose in redemption mirrors God's purpose in creation. "He who created us has Himself recreated us and prepared us for renewal in the fullness of holiness and righteousness in God."[8]

Charles Wesley saw as central to the Christian message that Jesus was "Born his Creatures to restore."[9] Restoration is not mere leniency or even acquittal. Edwin Lewis, in *A Christian Manifesto,* wrote that in Christ's incarnation, "divinity appeared within humanity and experienced its worst limitations that thereby humanity might lay hold upon divinity and find its salvation." For Edwin Lewis, "God-in-Christ-that-Christ-may-be-in-us" is the essential core of our faith.[10] In this he echoes St. Athanasius, for whom the purpose of the incarnation was "the sanctification of humanity."[11]

> For Athanasius the key to Christian salvation was that "He became what we are to make us what He is." By faith and by the work of the Holy Spirit, Christ not only covers human sin but also recovers the Divine Image (Gen 1:26) in which all humans were created. Hence, God becomes incarnate to transform Christians and allow them to become "partakers of the Divine nature" (2 Pet 1:4). Salvation is . . . nothing less than having the Divine nature (image of God) restored within humans, so that we are "in Christ" and

---

6. Matthew the Poor, *Titles of Christ,* 62.

7. Irenaeus, in Richardson, *Early Christian Fathers,* 386.

8. Matthew the Poor, *Communion of Love,* 148; 163.

9. Baker, *Hymns for the Nativity,* Hymn III, vv. 4, 6, 7.

10. Lewis, *Christian Manifesto,* 64; 51.

11. Tyson, *Great Athanasius,* 105.

"Christ is in us," and we become "new creatures" (2 Co 5:17) from the inside out.[12]

As Thomas F. Torrance wrote, "He condescends to enter into our human nature and so elevates it into union with his own divine nature. That is what took place in the incarnation of the Word, in the midst of Israel, in the midst of mankind."[13] Philip Sheldrake also makes this essential connection when he says, "In Christ, the outpouring of this divine life has as its end, or purpose, our deification or sharing in God's life."[14] B. F. Westcott, in his commentary on 1 John, wrote, "The image in which we were made will then be consummated in the likeness to which it was the divine purpose that we should attain."[15]

Similarly, for Catholic theologian Andrew Hofer, "Divinization and Incarnation are two sides of the same coin. For just as God came to share in our humanity, so we come to share in his divinity."[16] David Fagerberg quotes the *Catechism of the Catholic Church*: "The Word became flesh to make us partakers in the divine nature and of eternal life."[17] Pope Shenouda III conveys the same point: "The Lord Who has taken the weakness of our human nature, blessed this nature, and will grant to it transformation and glory in the General Resurrection."[18]

For John Wesley also, the purpose of Christ's coming is

> a restoration of man . . . to all that the old serpent deprived him of; a restoration not only to the favour, but likewise to the image of God; implying not barely deliverance from sin but the being filled with the fullness of God. It is plain . . . that nothing short of this is Christian religion.[19]

In "An Earnest Appeal to Men of Reason and Religion," Wesley challenged his readers to see the folly and emptiness of accepting our imperfect, "perishable world" as the limit of our hope:

---

12. Tyson, *Great Athanasius*, 173.

13. Walker, *Thomas F. Torrance, incarnation*, 45.

14. Sheldrake, *Spaces for the Sacred*, 67; cf. Tyson, *Great Athanasius*, 3.

15. Westcott, *Epistles of St. John*, 99.

16. Hofer, *Divinization*, 9.

17. David Fagerberg, in Hofer, *Divinization*, 22.

18. Shenouda III, "Holy Transfiguration," 10.

19. Wesley, "The End of Christ's Coming," in Outler, *Works of John Wesley*, 2:482–83.

> Once more, can you or any man of reason think you was [sic] made for the life you now live? You cannot possibly think so: at least, not till you tread the Bible under foot. The oracles of God bear thee witness in every page (and thine own heart agreeth thereto) that thou wast made in the image of God, an incorruptible picture of the God of glory. And what art thou even in thy present state? An everlasting spirit, going to God. For what end then did he create thee but to dwell with him above this perishable world, to know him, to love him, to do his will, to enjoy him for ever and ever![20]

In his sermon "The Image of God," Wesley describes in what ways (understanding, freedom, love) humanity was created in God's image, how that creation was marred by the fall, and how it is being restored in Christ.[21] Going far beyond "the constricted horizons of an exclusively juridical theology," like the Eastern Fathers, Wesley preaches a theology of transformation via "not only the justification, but also the restoration of creation in Christ."[22]

The medieval Irish theologian John Scottus Eriugena (c. 810–877) made the necessary connection between Jesus' incarnation and our grace-empowered transformation:

> The Word became flesh so that the flesh, that is, the human race, should ascend to him believing in the Word through the flesh, so that through the natural, only-begotten Son many should be adopted as sons. Not for his own sake did the Word become flesh, but for our sake, who could not be changed into the sons of God except by the flesh of the Word. He came down alone but ascends with many. He who made of God a human being makes gods of men and women. *And dwelt among us*, that is he took possession of our nature so that he might make us participators in his own nature."[23]

The fact that this Irish theologian could use familiar terms from Eastern writers reflects Ireland's early participation in the desert-inspired monastic movement, the universality of essential Christian theology, and Eriugena's work in translating such Eastern Fathers as Dionysius the Pseudo Areopagite, Gregory of Nyssa, and Maximus the Confessor.[24]

20. Wesley, "Earnest Appeal," in Cragg, *Works of John Wesley*, 11:62.

21. Outler, *Works of John Wesley*, 4:292–303.

22. Lossky, *Image and Likeness of God*, 102.

23. Eriugena, in Davies and O'Loughlin, *Celtic Spirituality*, 430; italics his.

24. Cross and Livingstone, *Oxford Dictionary of the Christian Church*, 468.

Archimandrite George conveys the sweep of grace in our lives from the fall, where through "egotism and self-assertion" our ancestors "separated themselves from God, and instead of attaining Theosis, they attained exactly the opposite; spiritual death." But "with the incarnation of the Logos [Christ], a second communion between God and humanity is realized." In Christ, by grace, God provides the way to the new creation.[25]

"The incarnation of the Logos and the theosis of man are the great mystery of our theology,"[26] George adds. Charles Wesley put it this way in one of his Nativity Hymns:

> He deigns in flesh t'appear,
> Widest extremes to join,
> To bring our vileness near,
> And make us all divine;
> And we the Life of GOD shall know,
> For GOD is manifest below.[27]

To become like Christ (1 John 3:2) is another way of seeing human destiny in light of transfigured glory, in continuity with transformation in this life. I. Howard Marshall says,

> John does not state explicitly in what new ways we shall be like Jesus at the parousia. But we may assume that the privileges which we now enjoy in an partial manner will then be ours fully and completely. Not only so, but we may also recollect that our hope is to see Jesus in his glory (Jn. 17:1, 5, 24) and therefore our hope is to share his glory, a hope that is clearly expressed by Paul (Rom. 8:18–19; Phil. 3:21; Col. 3:4) The process of glorification, already begun here and now in the lives of believers (2 Cor. 3:18) will reach completion."[28]

Beginning with the incarnation, every part of Jesus' ministry—his teaching and example, his miracles and compassion, his transfiguration and death, his resurrection and ascension, his Great Commission and sending of the Holy Spirit—flows from God's ultimate purpose for humanity, the restoration of the divine image in us within the new creation. Thus, very specifically, there is a clear, indispensable connection between

25. George, *Theosis*, 26, 27, 29; Cf. Ware, *Orthodox Way*, 74.

26. George, *Theosis*, 37.

27. Wesley, *Hymns for the Nativity*, Hymn VI, vv. 5, 15.

28. Marshall, *Epistles of John*, 172.

his incarnation and transfiguration. This pivotal event is not an isolated wonder, designed merely to impress Peter, James, John, and those who would follow. Nor does it reveal the depth of Jesus' identity apart from his redemptive mission. Rather, the transfiguration reveals both Jesus' indescribable glory and his intention to share that glory with us (John 17:19–24; Col 3:4).

# Chapter 4 _____

# Like the Sun:
# Visions of Destiny in Christ

There he was transfigured before them. His face shone like the sun, and his clothes became as white as the light.

—Matt 17:2 NIV

God's banners fly o'er us; God's light goes before us, a pillar of fire shining forth in the night, till shadows have vanished and darkness is banished, as forward we travel from light into light.

— Katherine K. Davis, *"Let All Things Now Living"*

Eternal light, shine into our hearts,

Eternal Goodness, deliver us from evil,

Eternal Power, be our support,

Eternal Wisdom, scatter the darkness of our ignorance,

Eternal pity, have mercy upon us;

that with all our heart and mind and soul and strength

we may seek your face

and be brought by your infinite mercy into your presence;

through Jesus Christ our Lord.

—Alcuin of York, Duffy, *Heart in Pilgrimage*

... your Heavenly Kingdom from which pain and lamentations are excluded, and where your chosen ones rejoice in everlasting happiness, illuminated through your Divine Glory.

—*The Rituals of the Armenian Apostolic Church*

The more the outward man decays,
The inner feels Thy strengthening grace,
And knows that Thou art mine:
Partaker of my glorious hope,
I here shall after Thee wake up,
Shall in Thine image shine.
—Charles Wesley, "For One in a Declining State of Health"

FOR MOST OF US, the transfiguration is, or can be, a sign of hope, a window to eternity, a revelation of Jesus' identity and a promise of our destiny as his people. Like those who received Paul's Letter to the Colossians, we can actually share "in the inheritance of his holy people in the kingdom of light," not because of our own accomplishments, but because "he has rescued us from the kingdom of darkness" (Col 1:12–13). But some believers throughout the ages have been swept up in an *immediate* experience of the divine light. One of those was St. Columba, the Irish monk who founded the great monastery on the island of Iona in Scotland. This is the way his hagiographer, Adomnan, described an experience of Columba as he was praying on the island of Hinba:

> During that time he remained day and night locked in his house, which was filled with heavenly light. No one was allowed to go near him, and he neither ate nor drank. But from the house rays of brilliant light could be seen at night, escaping through the chinks of the doors and though the keyholes. He was also heard singing spiritual chants of a kind never heard before.[1]

Orthodox writers mention examples of holy people, often monks, radiating divine light. Vladimir Lossky says that "According to St. Macarius of Egypt, the fire of grace kindled in the hearts of Christians by the Holy Spirit makes them shine like tapers before the Son of God."[2] Matthew the Poor says,

> Since the transfiguration day, Christ has not ceased to pour out His light on the bodies and faces of His saints. The wilderness of Scete is witness to this fact, and has won an abundant share in

1. Adomnan of Iona, *Life of St Columba*, III 18, 220.
2. Lossky, *Mystical Theology*, 219.

receiving the celestial light. . . . In these and other instances of luminous faces and bodies we can only see a true extension of the transfiguration of Christ . . . preparing them for the transfiguration and resurrection to come.[3]

Such accounts are hard for most contemporary Christians to imagine, or perhaps even to accept, yet they are consistent with the implications of the transfiguration. Some have seen them as extraordinary examples of "Christ in you, the hope of glory" (Col 1:27 NIV). Even if we take them as purely symbolic of certain people's progress in holiness and proximity to God, they testify to the ongoing work of the light of Christ in our world.

In a similar way, Charles Wesley wrote of observable light shining within and from those being transformed by grace: "Change my nature into thine, *'In me thy whole image shine.'*" Similarly, "And then throughout my nature shine, / And fill my soul with light divine." Wesley even provides an example of Mary Horton, who visibly radiated the light of Christ as she drew closer and closer to God.[4] Expanding on this theme in Wesley, Kimbrough says,

> One can see that partaking of the divine nature has a visible result. There is an inward and outward bearing of God's image, for his indwelling conveys all of God's purity, holiness, and love, which the one moving toward deification now personifies. Human beings radiate the image of God in the quest for holiness. Darkness is transformed into light through such radiance.[5]

The transfiguration is only one place in Scripture where shining like the sun appears. In John's vision at the beginning of Revelation, Jesus' "face was like the sun shining in all its brilliance" (Rev 1:16 NIV). When John writes that "God is light; in him there is no darkness at all," he builds upon a longstanding theme of light imagery used for God, as well as the Christian imperative that we should live in the light and be filled with the light (1 John 1:5; Matt 5:16; 6:11). Thus Jesus says "I am the light of the world. Whoever follows me will never walk in darkness, but will have the light of life" (John 8:12 NIV). Yet in another place, he tells his disciples, "You are the light of

---

3. Matthew the Poor, *Communion of Love*, 202–3; Cf. Meinardus, *Two Thousand Years*, 112–18.

4. Charles Wesley, in Kimbrough, *Partakers of the Life Divine*, 107, with Kimbrough's italics; 111; 109–10.

5. Kimbrough, *Partakers of the Life Divine*, 105; Cf. Sakharov, *We Shall See Him*, 59, 61.

the world," meaning that they (and we) must be filled to overflowing with his light (Matt 5:14 NIV). Paul encounters Christ in the "light from heaven, brighter than the sun, blazing around me and my companions" on the road to Damascus (Acts 26:13 NIV). In that experience, Jesus sends Paul on his mission to the gentiles, "to open their eyes and turn them from darkness to light" (Acts 26:18 NIV).

In the Old Testament Psalms, God's presence is "the light of your face." Someone God saves from enemies can "walk before God in the light of life." To one who trusts in God, "The Lord is my light and my salvation." Wisdom, goodness, and protection come from God, "For with you is the fountain of life; in your light we see light." God's word is "a lamp to my feet and a light for my path" (Ps 4:6; 56:13; 27:1; 36:9; 119:105 NIV).

The great blessing entrusted to "Aaron and his sons," asks that "The Lord make his face shine on you and be gracious to you" (Num 6:25 NIV). In a vision taken up later in Revelation, Isaiah sees a time when "The sun will no more be your light by day, nor will the brightness of the moon shine on you, for the Lord will be your everlasting light, and your God will be your glory" (Isa 60:19; Rev 21:23; 22:5 NIV). Light imagery in the prophetic books often conveys hope, and darkness its absence, as in Isaiah 9:2, "The people walking in darkness have seen a great light," or Micah 7:8, "Though I sit in darkness, the Lord will be my light" (NIV).

There is a future dimension to the light of Christ. In Matthew, at the end of the parable of the weeds, Jesus promises there will come a time when "the righteous will shine like the sun in the kingdom of their Father," a verse that reminds us of the promise in Daniel that "Those who are wise will shine like the brightness of the heavens, and those who lead many to righteousness, like the stars for ever and ever" (Matt 13:43; Dan 12:3 NIV). This theme appears again in Philippians, where Paul urges Christians to become "blameless and pure, children of God without fault in a warped and crooked generation. Then you will shine among them like stars in the sky as you hold firmly to the word of life" (Phil 2:15–16 NIV). This time the future is brought closer to the present. Indeed, heaven is both home to and source of "an eternal ocean of light."[6]

In the New Testament, Christ appeared to Paul in flashing light on the road to Damascus and commissioned him to be "a light for the Gentiles" (Acts 13:47; Isa 49:6 NIV). Later, Paul would connect the light of Christ with the light shining in Christians: "For God, who said, 'Let light shine

6. John of Dalyatha, in Matthew the Poor, *Orthodox Prayer Life*, 79.

35

out of darkness,' made his light shine in our hearts to give us the light of the knowledge of God's glory displayed in the face of Christ" (2 Cor 4:6; 1 Thess 5:5 NIV). He described the Ephesians, after their conversion, as "light in the Lord," encouraging them to "live as children of light" (Eph 5:8 NIV). In a similar way, Peter reminds his readers that God had "called you out of darkness into his wonderful light" (1 Pet 2:9 NIV). Second Peter compares God's word in Scripture to "a light shining in a dark place" (2 Pet 1:19 NIV).

The light the disciples saw in Jesus' face no doubt expressed all these dimensions of light—truth and wisdom, goodness and righteousness, clarity instead of confusion, hope instead of fear, and the transforming presence of God. All of these are then to be reflected in the lives of Jesus' followers and radiated into the darkness of the world. "In him was life, and that life was the light of all mankind. The light shines in the darkness, and the darkness has not overcome it" (John 1:4–5 NIV). In fact, "the whole creation is called to be penetrated through and through by the 'glory' of God."[7]

That same light was meant to shine through us. "Jesus . . . shines from within," when we shine—"like stars in the sky" or someday "like the sun in the kingdom"—it will be with the same light, but reflected[8] (Phil 2:15; Mat 13:43 NIV). On the one hand, we are called, like John the Baptist, "to testify concerning that light," for we, in our own way, "have seen his glory" (John 1:7, 14 NIV). But more than that, we are called to "reflect the Lord's glory," as we "are being transformed into his image with ever-increasing glory" (2 Cor 3:18 NIV). In this life, the accuracy of that reflection and the extent of that "ever-increasing glory" will always be a work in progress. Even so, we are encouraged to progress as those who "participate in the divine nature" (2 Pet 1:4 NIV).

Commenting on the disciples in Matthew's transfiguration account, Dorothy Lee says, "the transfiguration is for their benefit and ultimately for their transfiguration." Drawn to God's light and glory, "Jesus calls them to participate in his own metamorphosis where, like him, they will one day 'shine like the sun in the kingdom of their Father' (13:43)."[9] Irenaeus of Lyons said, "Those who see light are within light, and share the brilliance of the light. Just so, those who see God are within God and receive of his splendor, a radiance of the vision of God that gives us life."[10] Since light is

---

7. Monk of the Eastern Church, *Orthodox Spirituality*, 97.

8. Ratzinger, *Eschatology*, 310.

9. Lee, *Transfiguration*, 58.

10. Irenaeus, "Against the Heresies," in McGuckin, *Book of Mystical Chapters*, 121.

characteristic of God, light should be characteristic of God's people. "Our faces become the faces in which the resurrected Christ shows forth his beauty and his glory."[11]

In the next life, the progress is revealed to be astounding, beyond our imagination: "Dear friends, now we are children of God, and what we will be has not yet been made known. But we know that when Christ appears, we shall be like him, for we shall see him as he is" (1 John 3:2 NIV). As Daniel Keating notes, "It is by beholding the Lord as he is that we are changed into his very image. We are to be sons and daughters who are like the Son."[12] One of the Wesleys' favorite early Christian writers spoke of the implications of the transfiguration for us: "As the body of the Lord was glorified when he climbed the mount and was transfigured into the divine glory and into infinite light, so also the bodies of the saints are glorified and shine like lightning."[13] As Dorothy Lee puts it, "Through the transfiguration, the destiny of believers is to share in the nature and glory of God."[14] Charles Wesley prayed, "The promise stands for ever sure, And we shall in thine image shine."[15]

Archimandrite George of Mount Athos distinguishes this transformation from a much more limited moral improvement: "The purpose of our life is not just that man should become better than he is, more moral, more just, more self-controlled, more mindful; all these must happen, but none of them are the great purpose, the ultimate purpose for which our Maker and Creator moulded man." We realize that purpose through "not only an external, moral relationship, but a personal union with [our] Creator." Changes in our attitudes and behavior toward life and other people come as a result of our transformation; it is only our union with God that fulfills our destiny. "Having been endowed 'in His image,' man is called upon to be completed in His likeness.' This is Theosis. The Creator, God by nature, calls men to become a god by Grace." Therefore, "since man is 'called to be a god' (i.e. was created to become a god), as long as he does not find himself on the path of *Theosis* he feels an emptiness within himself."[16]

---

11. Graham, *Where I Am*, 60.

12. Keating, *Deification and Grace*, 18.

13. Macarius, Homily 15:38, in Maloney, *Pseudo-Macarius*, 122.

14. Lee, *Transfiguration*, 96.

15. Charles Wesley, in Hildebrandt and Beckerlegge, *Works of John Wesley*, 7:540.

16. George, *Theosis*, 21–22.

There is a powerful musical version of John's vision in a song written by Jennie Lee Riddle and Jonathan Lee, called "When the Stars Burn Down" (Cf. 1 John 3:2 and Rev 4:11; 5:12; 7:12). Though I quote only part, I encourage you listen to the entire song. You may well be moved to join in the chorus:

> There will come a day, standing face to face
> In a moment we'll be like Him.
> He will wipe our eyes dry and take us up to His side
> And forever we will be His.
> Singing "Blessing and honor and glory and power forever to our God."[17]

In the words of Nikolaos Vassiliadis, "It is for this kingdom that we have experienced a nostalgia ever since we were exiled from earthly paradise." It is fascinating and highly appropriate to speak of our longing for God's kingdom as "nostalgia," since the new creation is indeed a restoration of its original (for John Wesley, it is even better!). Nor are these superficially "pious desires. For the deification of man was the purpose of the whole of divine creation, and the ultimate truth of man."[18] Matthew the Poor speaks of "the Kingdom for which we were born, and the eternal homeland to which we were called."[19] For "Christ is the Morning Star, who when the night of this world is past brings to his saints the promise of the light of life and opens [to them] the everlasting day."[20]

Commenting on 1 John 3:2, Vassiliadis says "'we shall see Him as He is' in the state of divine glory which will be reflected and will shine in us as in spiritual mirrors."[21] Thomas Torrance writes similarly: "And faith knows that day will come when Jesus Christ, the incarnate Son of God, will return and the veil will be torn asunder and we shall see him as he is and become like him."[22] Bede's comment on this verse clarifies "like him," along with John's statement that "we are the sons of God," by saying, "When we fully enjoy the contemplation of the immutable and eternal Divinity, we too shall be immortal and eternal in him; we shall not be the same as he, but similar,

---

17. Riddle and Lee, "When the Stars Burn Down."
18. Vassiliadis, *Mystery of Death*, 539; 545.
19. Matthew the Poor, *Words for Our Lives*, 68.
20. Bede, in J. Robert Wright, *Companion to Bede*, 4.
21. Vassiliadis, *Mystery of Death*, 550.
22. Walker, *Thomas F. Torrance, incarnation*, 344.

because we are his creature."[23] Ephrem the Syrian included this vision in one of his Hymns on Paradise:

> The Lord of all
> the treasure store of all things:
> upon each according to his capacity
> He bestows a glimpse of His hiddenness,
> of the splendor of His Majesty.
> He is the radiance who, in his love,
> makes everyone shine.[24]

Even in this life there have been those who have experienced God's light in figurative and even literal ways. One of these, the monk Sophrony Sakharov, describes his experience in this way:

> Over and over again my heart would sing praises to Christ-God Who manifests Himself in Uncreated Light. Thus incalculably powerful, beyond all bounds, He descends to us. The inviolable, searchless Light of His Divinity quickens and embraces all that exists. Notions of place, of volume, do not apply, and yet non-spacially His Light is everywhere. To be illumined by this Light brings an experience of resurrection, a foretaste of bliss to come. Wordlessly the Light tells our spirit that, "made in His image" [Cf. Gen. 1:26], in his final consummation man will appear as the bearer of the fullness of God-man life, will be perfected after the likeness of Christ, God-and-man.[25]

Matthew the Poor wrote of the transfigured appearance of early monastics in the Egyptian desert as part of "the whole creation . . . groaning in travail together" for a transformation "not only of our bodies," but of the entire created order. This light in the desert anticipates the final, universal triumph of light. He makes it clear that Christ's transfiguration was meant to be shared with his people, and that several desert fathers visibly radiated the light of Christ.[26] Examples included:

> St Macarius the Great, whose body was "shining in the darkness inside his cell", St Sesoes, whose face radiated "with a light that gradually increased until he gave up the spirit", Abba Pambo,

23. Bede, in Van Der Pas, *Glossa Ordinaria*, 30.

24. Brock, *St. Ephrem the Syrian*, Hymn IX:25, 145.

25. Sakharov, *We Shall See Him*, 186; Cf. 209.

26. Davis, *Coptic Christology in Practice*, 274–75.

whose face was difficult to gaze upon "because of the glory that shone from him", St Arsenius, whose disciples found his whole body "alight like fire", and St. Joseph the Great, whose fingers "looked like ten flames of fire" when he was praying.[27]

Matthew the Poor also makes the connection between such experiences and the transfiguration itself. Such experiences should not be thought of as isolated spectacles, but as signs pointing to the transfiguration itself and the promised transfiguration of God's people. "In these and other instances of luminous faces and bodies we can only see a true extension of the transfiguration of Christ . . . preparing them for the transfiguration and resurrection to come."[28] Testimonies like these and that of Adomnan regarding Columba of Iona, mentioned earlier, may be difficult for many to accept, yet they point to a reality that is not at all dependent on such stories, the reality well attested in Scripture that in some mysterious way, "the Lord Jesus Christ, who by the power that enables him to bring everything under his control, will transform our lowly bodies so that they will be like his glorious body" (Phil 3:21 NIV). Paul's vision and promise point to the future, yet the transfiguration may also break in to our present reality in ways that are unexpected and inexpressible.

Basic to an appreciation of God's light and glory is an awareness of God as mystery—a reality partly revealed, yet always beyond our understanding. In the words of Sophrony Sakharov,

> Our Father dwells "in the light which no man can approach" [I Tim. 6:16]. Invariably He remains a great mystery to us, even when we are filled with a sense of His nearness. But man, too, created in the image of the All-Highest, is also a precious enigma and we must never cease trying to learn more and more about him and the loftiness of his calling "before the foundation of the world" [John 17:24].[29]

Thus it should not be surprising that mystery is foundational to Charles Wesley's approach to God and to the path of transformation. Combining mystery and humility, "Wesley is awestruck by the expression of divine love toward him and all humankind and knows indubitably that no one deserves such love.[30] As he sings of this "great salvation," of human

27. Matthew the Poor, in Davis, *Coptic Christology in Practice*, 274.

28. Matthew the Poor, *Communion of Love*, 202, 203.

29. Sakharov, *We Shall See Him*, 24.

30. Kimbrough, *Partakers of the Life Divine*, 10.

beings "changed from glory into glory, till in heaven we take our place," Wesley joins those heavenly beings who "cast their crowns before thee, lost in wonder, love, and praise."[31]

For Dorothy Lee, "The Transfiguration on the mountain is the meeting-place between human beings and God, between the temporal and the eternal, between past, present and future, between everyday human life—with all its hopes and fears—and the mystery of God." The meeting place on that mountain allowed the three disciples to see and enter the reality of their Lord in a way they could not understand, but could not forget. In time, they would come to know that Jesus "is the point of intersection, the bridge between heaven and earth, the source of hope, bringing to birth—through incarnation, death, and resurrection, God's eschatological future."[32]

Transfiguration in Christ begins and can be seen in this life in people who show creative genius and inspiration, who are transformed and empowered by gifts of the Spirit, whose wisdom is extraordinary, or who face the ordeal of martyrdom with astounding grace. Pope Shenouda spoke of "certain dreams" in which "we see a person whom we know, in a wonderful image or in a brilliant form, although we do not see him like this in his earthly life. But he appears to you during the dream in a state of transfiguration."[33] I would contend that there are also times of intense wakefulness when we can see another person—very much within this life—in that same way. At such times we can perceive God at work in that person's life. We see in them an unmistakable spiritual depth, and we catch a momentary glimpse of the destiny toward which that person is headed. In a moment of inspired worship, teaching, generosity, or compassion, the light of Christ shines forth, sometimes visibly and tangibly. Nevertheless,

> All the cases of transfiguration on the earth—whether for a moment or in a permanent way—are nothing but the pledge of the eternal transfiguration in the kingdom; these cases are simply a taste of the kingdom, and the gifts of the richness of the glory of God."[34]

---

31. Charles Wesley, "Love Divine, All Loves Excelling," *United Methodist Hymnal*, #384, v. 4.

32. Lee, *Transfiguration*, 2.

33. Shenouda III, "Holy Transfiguration," 15.

34. Shenouda III, "Holy Transfiguration," 15.

# Chapter 5 _____

# "Glory Into Glory": Transfiguration and Sanctification in the Theology of John and Charles Wesley

Finish, then, thy new creation; pure and spotless let us be. Let us see thy great salvation perfectly restored in thee; changed from glory into glory, till in heaven we take our place, till we cast our crowns before thee, lost in wonder, love, and praise.
—Charles Wesley, "Love Divine, All Loves Excelling"

Let my whole being be filled with your light so that others may be drawn to you.
—Michael Buckley, *Heart in Pilgrimage*

Made like him, like him we rise, Alleluia!
—"Christ the Lord Is Risen Today" *The United Methodist Hymnal*

Eastern Orthodoxy and the Wesleys' theology are natural conversation partners because they drink from the same stream, and both are returning to their respective traditions.
—Michael J. Christensen, *Partakers of the Divine Nature*

This perfection is the restoration of man to the state of holiness from which he fell, by creating him anew in Christ Jesus, and restoring to him that image and likeness of God which he has lost.
—Adam Clarke, *Christian Theology*

IT IS FITTING TO place the theology and spirituality of John and Charles Wesley within the broadly ecumenical context from which they drew, and to understand their teaching on the way of salvation in dialogue with the Great Tradition. Key to the Wesleys' theology is "the transforming power of grace."[1] Their thought on this transformation was based in the New Testament, the early church, and their own Anglican tradition, among others.[2]

Sanctifying grace was at the forefront of the Wesleys' writing, organization, and leadership. While they had other theological concerns, they saw the essence of Christianity as the life of grace toward Christian perfection. "The doctrine of Christian perfection is not simply one among others for Wesley." Instead, it "occupies a center stage in Wesley's theology because perfection is the goal of the Christian life."[3] In their orthodoxy and in their commitment to the way of salvation, they represent not an ecclesiastical backwater, but the very center of ecumenical Christianity. Drawing their thought and practice from many streams in the Great Tradition, within and beyond their own Anglicanism, they built a movement around the appropriation of transfiguring grace. Along with the New Testament, they were especially drawn to the teaching and spirituality of the Eastern fathers. Michael Ramsey wrote of *his* perspective, " . . . my own theological thinking became more Eastern than Western. The New Testament and the Greek Fathers came to be the medium in which I thought, together with such Anglican Divines as had themselves been influenced by Greek theology."[4] Ramsey's description could easily apply to John and Charles Wesley.[5] Thus Wesley scholar Theodore Runyan speaks of the influence of "the Greek and Syrian Fathers of the first five centuries of the Christian era . . . on Wesley's theology."[6] In this they were not alone, for surrounding the Wesleys was a deep thirst among Anglicans for ancient sanctification theology.[7]

Thomas Merton once wrote that "For each of us, there is only one thing necessary, to fulfill our own destiny, according to God's will, to be what God wants us to be."[8] In sanctifying grace, the Holy Spirit empowers

1. Oden, *Transforming Power of Grace.*

2. Collins, *Partaking in Divine Nature,* 152–56. For writers who influenced Wesley and Wesleyan theology, see Maddox, *Responsible Grace,* 250; 372n140.

3. Colon-Emeric, *Wesley, Aquinas, and Christian Perfection,* 11.

4. Ramsey, in Rowell, "Michael Ramsey, Transfiguration," in Dales, *Glory Descending,* 201.

5. See Kimbrough, "Window," in Newport and Campbell, *Charles Wesley,* 180.

6. Runyan, *New Creation,* 13.

7. Kimbrough, *Partakers of the Life Divine,* 5.

8. Thomas Merton, in Coniaris, *Achieving Your Potential in Christ,* 102.

the transformation that makes this destiny possible. The content and trajectory of this transformation is love, which is for the Wesleys the nature and character of God. "Love is who God is; love is what God is like; and love is the way in which God's self-disclosure is revealed."[9] Charles prayed, "Change my nature into thine, / In me thy whole image shine."[10] That shining image is the manifestation of God's love, reflected and reciprocated in our relationship with him.

> For to this end was man created, to love God; and to this end alone, even to love the Lord his God with all his heart, soul, mind, and strength. But love is the very image of God: it is the brightness of his glory. *By love man is not only made like God, but in some sense one with him.*"[11]

At times the promise of transfiguration seems to be limited to a select few, often certain monastics, who leave the world behind in order to make themselves fully available to sanctifying grace. In this view, an ascetic way of life seeks to conquer the sinful nature through rigorous spiritual discipline, separate from the world. Others, especially John and Charles Wesley and the movement they initiated, set forth a kind of democratized vision with its own discipline, but keep it more accessible, situated in the midst of the world, designed for a multitude.

It would, however, be a mistake to make too sharp a distinction among traditions. For example, Norman Russell, writing about *theosis* in Orthodox tradition, sees this experience as "intended for all believers without exception."[12] Similarly, Kallistos Ware writes, "Deification is not something reserved for a few select initiates, but something intended for all alike."[13] Anglican theologian A. M. Allchin sees the transforming personal encounter with God as "that common Christian experience of the mysteries of the faith, which is open in some degree to everyone who believes," and sees the Wesleys as proponents of that encounter within the context of ancient

---

9. Kimbrough, *Partakers of the Life Divine*, 91.

10. Charles Wesley, in Kimbrough, *Partakers of the Life Divine*, 97.

11. John Wesley, in Kimbrough, *Partakers of the Life Divine*, 87 (Kimbrough's italics); See also Wesley's tract "Plain Account of Christian Perfection" and related documents in Chilcote and Collins, *Works of John Wesley*, 13:1–199.

12. Russell, *Fellow Workers with God*, 169.

13. Kallistos Ware, in Keating, *Deification and Grace*, 61.

tradition.[14] Thomas Aquinas believed that "all Christians, clergy and lay, are called to perfection."[15]

For Coptic theologian Matthew the Poor, "Even as Egyptian monks stand as the vanguard and model for the enactment of the divine life, such 'incarnational participation' is made available to laypersons through the ritual practices of worship."[16] For all the human limitations of people and churches, "the Church has the divine capacity attained through Christ to make every single person one with God."[17] John Meyendorff points out that "The main concern of [Gregory] Palamas is to affirm that this goal is not reserved to isolated 'mystics', but is, in fact, identical with Christian faith itself and, therefore, offered to all the members of the Church, in virtue of their baptism."[18] So while the Wesleys and their movement successfully popularized, democratized, and organized the doctrine and experience of sanctification, their work was rooted in a very long and ecumenical tradition.[19]

Foundational to all of this is the primacy of transforming grace. Kevin Watson has rightly said that "we are not, and cannot be, the source of our own transformation. Sanctification is a sheer act of grace. We cannot earn it or merit it. It is freely given to us by the Triune God."[20] The transformation of human character is, from start to finish, God's gift of grace. "The goal is transformation, and in all of this we are dependent upon the grace of God to become who he created us to be."[21] The Wesleys' emphasis on grace as the indispensable power for transformation echoes the ancient Letter to Diognetus, for "when we had shown ourselves incapable of entering the Kingdom of God by our own efforts, we might be made capable of doing so by the power of God."[22] Andreas Andreopoulos says of our utter dependence on grace:

> Within the limitations of our nature, we have no more hope of reaching God than a mad boatman in the night who hopes to row all the way to the moon that is reflected on the water. And yet,

14. Allchin, *Kingdom of Love and Knowledge*, 15.

15. Colon-Emeric, *Wesley, Aquinas, and Christian Perfection*, 151.

16. Davis, *Coptic Christology in Practice*, 275.

17. Matthew the Poor, *Communion of Love*, 217.

18. Palamas, *Gregory Palamas*, 8.

19. Cf. Coleson, *Be Holy*.

20. Watson, *Class Meeting*, 126.

21. Long, *Quest for Holiness*, xii.

22. Diognetus, in Richardson, *Early Christian Fathers*, 220.

the miracle of the Transfiguration shows us that the grace of God covers the distance.[23]

Coptic monk Matthew the Poor painted a vivid picture of humanity "transposed from a dead decaying nature to a new and divine one."[24] In the Wesleys' vision, this transformation affects each Christian's body, character, and destiny. It is a spiritual reality with physical and moral results leading to God's eternal kingdom. John Wesley asked with great urgency,

> . . . can you or any man of reason think you was (sic) made for the life you now lead? You cannot possibly think so: at least, not till you tread the Bible under foot. The oracles of God bear thee witness in every page (and thine own heart agreeth thereto) that thou wast made in the image of God, an incorruptible picture of the God of glory. And what art thou even in thy present state? An everlasting spirit, going to God.[25]

Wesley juxtaposed the alternative to this vision of eternal life and growth:

> Or are you already convinced there is no hereafter? What a poor state then are you in now! Taking a few more dull turns upon earth, and then dropping into nothing! What kind of spirit must you be of if you can sustain yourself under the thought! Under the expectation of being in a few minutes swept away by the stream of time, and then for ever . . . swallowed up, and lost in the wide womb of uncreated night![26]

Sanctification or transformation in Christ is the whole point of conversion or justification for Wesley. As Anthony Coniaris puts it, "Theosis is the positive aspect of salvation."[27] Indeed, "Holiness and sanctification are not additions to justification, but its actualization."[28] Wesley goes well beyond forensic salvation to therapeutic salvation, salvation that heals, restores, and makes whole. Wesley called the transforming journey "the way to heaven" in the preface to his collection of sermons:

23. Andreopoulos, *This Is My Beloved Son*, 129.

24. Matthew the Poor, *Words for Our Lives*, 2:176.

25. John Wesley, "An Earnest Appeal to Men of Reason and Religion," in Cragg, *Works of John Wesley* 11:62.

26. John Wesley, "Earnest Appeal," in Cragg, *Works of John Wesley*, 11:72.

27. Coniaris, *Tools for Theosis*, 20.

28. Kharlamov, *Theosis*, 2:10.

I want to know one thing—the way to heaven—how to land safe on that happy shore. God himself has condescended to teach the way; for this very end he came from heaven. He hath written it down in a book. O give me that book! At any price, give me the book of God! I have it. Here is knowledge enough for me.[29]

The way to heaven is the path of sanctification, "the road to eternal life"[30] It is not merely a route, but a participation, a foretaste of things to come. It is not an escape, but an alignment of everyday life with ultimate destiny. This way recognizes the changes that must take place within us as we go. It provides not only direction, but power—bread for our journey, means of grace. The world is full of distractions and we are easily turned aside. What matters most is that we continue walking "the road to the kingdom of heaven."[31] Indeed we must "run with perseverance the race marked out for us" (Heb 12:1 NIV). With Paul we "press on toward the goal to win the prize for which God has called me heavenward in Christ Jesus" (Phil 3:14 NIV).

Wesleyan theology sees salvation not as a momentary transaction, but rather a panorama of transforming grace: "So that salvation which is here spoken of might be extended to the entire work of God, from the first dawning of grace in the soul till it is consummated in glory."[32] This is what Charles Wesley called "Thy Great Salvation" in "Love Divine, All Loves Excelling."[33] This salvation, realizable even now, gives us real and lasting hope. For the Wesleys,

> Salvation is more than a new perspective, more than a new relationship with the divine; it is the actual impartation of the divine reality to the individual by the Spirit, effecting a total change in thought and action. The eschatological goal may be brought into present experience, not in its full measure, but nonetheless, in its essential character.[34]

29. John Wesley, "Preface to Sermons," in Outler, *Works of John Wesley*, 1:105.

30. Casey, *Road to Eternal Life*.

31. à Kempis, *Imitation of Christ*, 121.

32. John Wesley, "The Scripture Way of Salvation," in Collins and Vickers, *Sermons of John Wesley*, 583.

33. *United Methodist Hymnal*, #384.

34. Bence, "John Wesley's Teleological Hermeneutic," 267.

John Oswalt says that "God's grace was meant not only to deliver us from the guilt of sin, but also from its power."[35] Salvation is not God's accommodation to the human condition, but his transformation of that condition in a way that prepares us for life in his kingdom, even as we taste that kingdom here (Rev 21:27).

> Christ's redemption of humanity not only reconciles God and humanity, it brings about the sanctification or deification (*theosis*) of those who believe and live by faith in Christ. This was stressed through Athanasius' famous dictum: "He became what we are to make us what He is."[36]

John Wesley approached the subject of heaven and life after death with humility, recognizing that while Scripture reveals important insights, heaven remains a mystery, only partly understood. In his sermon "The New Creation," Wesley admits this limitation:

> It must be allowed that after all the researches we can make, still our knowledge of the great truth which is delivered to us in these words is exceedingly short and imperfect. At this point of mere revelation, beyond the reach of our natural faculties, we cannot penetrate far into it, nor form any adequate conception of it. But it may be an encouragement to those who have in any degree tasted of the powers of the world to come to go as far as we can go, interpreting Scripture by Scripture, according to the analogy of faith.[37]

One of Wesley's conclusions was that the ultimate prize, the new creation, "will be even better than the paradise that Adam and Eve knew."[38] "Hence will arise an unmixed state of holiness and happiness far superior to that which Adam enjoyed in paradise."[39] Here Wesley reflects Macarius, who said that "man not only comes to the measure of the first Adam, but he also reaches a greater state than he possessed. For man is divinized."[40]

Charles Wesley, reflecting on the nativity of Christ, wrote:

> He deigns in flesh to appear,
> Widest extremes to join,

35. Oswalt, *Called to Be Holy*, 5.

36. Tyson, *Great Athanasius*, 22.

37. Outler, *Works of John Wesley*, 2:501.

38. Maddox, *Responsible Grace*, 253; Cf. Runyan, *New Creation*, 11.

39. John Wesley, "New Creation," in Collins, *Theology of John Wesley*, 326.

40. Macarius, in Maloney, *Pseudo-Macarius*, 164.

To bring our vileness near
And make us all divine;
And we the life of God shall know,
For God is manifest below.[41]

Consistent with his emphasis on the love of God and the commandment to love, John Wesley envisions the new creation as the completion of growth in love. "Perfect love, the restoration of the divine image in humanity within history, is an anticipatory expression of the final restoration beyond history."[42] We see the same emphasis in these lines from Charles:

Turn us again, O God, and shew
The Brightness of thy lovely Face,
So shall we all be Saints below,
And sav'd, and perfected in Grace.[43]

Heaven will continue and fulfill our experience of the kingdom in this life, and it will involve, for Wesley as for all of orthodox Christianity, the resurrection of the body.[44] For now, however, we can only glimpse that fulfillment from a distance. Wesley shared with Thomas à Kempis an awareness of human limitation in imagining or describing the reality of heaven, the eternal kingdom, the new creation:

Oh, that this day would dawn and all these passing things would come to an end! That day, indeed, shines upon the saints with resplendent and everlasting brightness. But to us who are still on our earthly pilgrimage, it is seen only from afar and as through a glass, darkly.[45]

Basing his ideas on Scripture and using his own theological method—the much misused "Wesley Quadrilateral"—Wesley was able to see a number of key elements in the human destiny God intends for his people. Perhaps chief among these is an extension of the way of growth toward perfection as we know it in this life. Randy Maddox points out that Wesley

---

41. Baker, *Hymns for the Nativity*, Hymn #VI, vv. 5, 15.

42. Oden, *John Wesley's Scriptural Christianity*, 358.

43. Charles Wesley in Tyson, *Charles Wesley: A Reader*, 400; Cf. Kimbrough, *Partakers of the Life Divine*, 42.

44. Maddox, *Responsible Grace*, 239, 240, 247–49.

45. à Kempis, *Imitation of Christ*, 140.

believed "growth in grace was so characteristic of the Christian life that the 'perfect' would continue to grow to all eternity."[46]

John Wesley believed that in the new creation, "all the earth shall then be a more beautiful paradise than Adam ever saw." In that new paradise "cruelty will be far away, and savageness and fierceness be forgotten. So that violence shall be heard no more, neither wasting or destruction seen on the face of the earth."[47] Included in Wesley's peaceful vision was a restored animal kingdom, where nature no longer functioned with predator and prey, and where animals had their own place in eternity.[48] "But the most glorious of all will be the change which then will take place on the poor, sinful, miserable children of men." God's people will enjoy "an unmixed state of holiness and happiness far superior to that which Adam enjoyed in paradise." Specifically, "there will be no more sin. And to crown all, there will be a deep, an intimate, and uninterrupted union with God; a constant communion with the Father and his Son Jesus Christ, through the Spirit; a continual enjoyment of the Three-One God, and of all the creatures in him!"[49]

This "uninterrupted communion with God," defined by love, was the goal of early Methodism's pursuit of Christian perfection, a goal which was to be lived out as far as possible even in this world.[50] Yet important as is the here and now, this world does not begin to exhaust grace-empowered growth toward God. Like the early fathers, the Wesleys envisioned endless progress in sanctification. Consistent with the thought of Gregory of Nyssa, they knew "the soul's ascent into God will never cease. The infinity of God implies that despite our growth in knowledge, God remains beyond our understanding." Gregory says, "the path that lies beyond our immediate grasp is infinite." Those who walk the road of God's infinite goodness "will always enjoy a greater and greater participation in grace throughout all eternity."[51] David Watson, paraphrasing John Wesley, says that "no matter how much we grow in our faith and love of God, we can still grow more.

---

46. Maddox, *Responsible Grace*, 253.

47. John Wesley, "New Creation," Outler, *Works of John Wesley*, 2:508–9.

48. Cf. Wesley's Sermon "General Deliverance," Outler, *Works of John Wesley*, 2:436–50; Cf. Romans 8:21.

49. John Wesley, "New Creation," Outler, *Works of John Wesley*, 2:509–10.

50. Flew, *Idea of Perfection*, 323; 324–25.

51. Gregory of Nyssa, in Boersma, *Heavenly Participation*, 162.

God never stops inviting us to journey more deeply into the divine life. God's love is an inexhaustible fountain."[52]

Charles Wesley stresses 2 Peter's promise that "you may participate in the divine nature" (2 Pet 1:4 NIV). For Charles, sharing the divine nature, like new birth, is made possible in us by grace. He was influenced in this by Henry Scougal, who wrote of "a real participation of the divine nature, the very image of God drawn upon the soul, or, in the apostle's phrase, 'It is Christ formed within us.'"[53] For Charles, humanity's original state at creation was as a participant in the divine nature, a state which is restored by God's new creation.[54]

> Dost thou not know what religion is? That it is the participation in the divine nature [II Pet 1:4], the life of God in the soul of man; "Christ in thee, the hope of glory" [Col 1:27]; "Christ formed in thy heart" [Gal 4:19], happiness and holiness; heaven begun on earth; a "kingdom of God within thee" [Cf. Luke 17:21] . . .?[55]

This prolific hymn writer devoted many verses to the related theme of perfection as participation, which he saw as the essential and ultimate purpose of Christian life. For Charles, faithful Christians are *Partakers of true holiness, / And filled with all the life divine.*"[56] He yearned for the day "When all renewed in love I shine, / *Partaker of the life divine.*"[57]

Adam Clarke, early Methodist Scripture scholar and theologian, wrote of heaven as the perfect destiny, where, "The soul is renewed in glory; the body fashioned after the glorious human nature of Jesus Christ; and both joined together in an indestructible bond, clearer than the indestructible moon, brighter than the sun, and more resplendent than all the heavenly spheres." Clarke spoke of eternal life as "the proper object of an immortal spirit's hope," where God "is SEEN AS HE IS; and where he can be enjoyed without interruption in an eternal progression of knowledge and beatitude."[58] Pope Shenouda says of this progression, "Thus is the human

---

52. Watson, *Scripture and the Life*, 30.

53. Henry Scougal, in Kimbrough, *Partakers of the Life Divine*, 17.

54. Kimbrough, *Partakers of the Life Divine*, 19 and 20.

55. Charles Wesley, "Awake, Thou that Sleepest," in Kimbrough, *Partakers of the Life Divine*, 21.

56. Kimbrough, *Partakers of the Life Divine*, 34 (italics his).

57. Kimbrough, *Partakers of the Life Divine*, 33 (italics his). He lived to be "perfected in love," and to *"live on earth the life divine"* (30, italics his).

58. Clarke, *Christian Theology*, 377 (caps his); Cf. Johnston, *Cloud of Unknowing*, 45.

nature in transfiguration: where it enters into the perpetual spiritual life, and in the spiritual pleasure which is the property of the sons of God."[59]

While he admits that "It is in vain to attempt to describe this state," Clarke is still clear about that which can be known or inferred from Scripture. For example, he believes that "extraordinary talents are not given merely in reference to this world," but continue into the next, where perfected humans, "eternally expand upon their powers in the service of Him from whom they derive their being."[60] Thus God intends for this to be a permanent part of our character, which will actually grow and flourish in our new and glorified existence.

The most compelling part of Clarke's portrait of heaven is its "endless sources of comfort and happiness," the polar opposite of stagnation, not in the sense of material pleasures, but rather of the spiritual growth begun in this life.[61] He describes "eternal living fountains" offering "an infinite variety in the enjoyments of the blessed."[62] Here is a vision of heaven that is anything but static or boring:

> There will be no sameness, and consequently no cloying with the perpetual enjoyment of the same things; every moment will open a new source of pleasure, instruction, and improvement; they shall make an eternal progression into the fullness of God. And as God is infinite, so his attributes are infinite; and throughout eternity more and more of those attributes will be discovered; and the discovery of each will be a new fountain or source of pleasure and enjoyment. These sources must be opening through all eternity; and yet, through all eternity, there will still remain, in the absolute perfections of the Godhead, an infinity of them to be opened![63]

For Clarke, these are the "eternal pleasures" (KJV: "pleasures for evermore"; Clarke: "ever and more") of "joy in your presence" promised to those who walk "the path of life" (Ps 16:11 NIV)—an "eternal progression in unadulterated, unchangeable, and unlimited happiness."[64] American Methodist Nathan Bangs echoed Clarke's vision, saying, "Yes, from that river, exhaustless as its Fountain, shall forever flow those streams, not only

59. Shenouda III, "Holy Transfiguration," 12.
60. Clarke, *Christian Theology*, 378–79.
61. Ibid., 379.
62. Ibid., 379.
63. Ibid., 379.
64. Ibid., 380.

of Divine joy, but of endless knowledge, which shall fill the soul with the purest pleasure and the most ecstatic delight."[65]

David Watson says of Christian growth in this life, "Even for people who have walked in faith for decades, there is still the opportunity to grow in faith, to enter more deeply into the eternal love that exists between the Father, Son, and Holy Spirit."[66] Clarke extends that vision to ever-expanding, never-ending growth toward God's eternity and infinity. There are no boundaries to hope beyond those we place in our own path.

This vision of eternal, infinite progress echoes Gregory of Nyssa's "Doctrine of Infinite Growth," commenting on Philippians 3:13:

> . . . the graces that we receive at every point are indeed great, but the path that lies beyond our immediate grasp is infinite. This will constantly happen to those who thus share in the divine Goodness, and they will always enjoy a greater and greater participation in grace throughout all eternity.[67]

Given such a vision, when someone "enters into the world of divine eternity," that person "is struck by the majesty of the vision opening before him."[68] Albert Outler said that for John Wesley, "'perfection' meant 'perfecting' (teleosis), with further horizons of love and participation in God always opening up beyond any level of spiritual progress."[69] The medieval author of *The Cloud of Unknowing* agreed that the process of transformation within ourselves and in our relationship with God "is a work that begins here on earth but will go on without end into eternity."[70] Again from Gregory of Nyssa: "For this is truly perfection: never to stop growing toward what is better and never placing any limit on perfection."[71] Behind this infinite growth is what John Meyendorff calls the "inexhaustible mystery of His being."[72]

In Wesleyan theology, "Each successive (present) moment of this process is . . . both an attainment of a measure of salvation and an invitation

---

65. Bangs, *Necessity, Nature, and Fruits*, 310.

66. Watson, *Scripture and the Life*, 125.

67. Gregory of Nyssa, in Musurillo, *From Glory to Glory*, 211–12.

68. Sakharov, *We Shall See Him*, 190.

69. Albert Outler, in Bence, "John Wesley's Teleological Hermeneutic," 172.

70. Johnston, *Cloud of Unknowing*, 188.

71. Gregory of Nyssa, On Perfection, in *Ancient Christian Commentary on Scripture*, 7:226.

72. Palamas, *Gregory Palamas*, 143.

to press forward to an even fuller realization of the good."[73] Wesley asked, "Can those who are perfect grow in grace? . . . Undoubtedly they can. And that not only while they are in the body, but to all eternity."[74]

John Meyendorff expressed similar sentiments when summarizing the thought of Gregory Palamas: "because God remains absolutely transcendent in His essence, man's communication with Him has no limit. It never reaches an End, which would be a dead end. God is both transcendent and inexhaustible."[75]

Matthew the Poor says in this regard: "Yet, however great the distance we cover along the way, fullness of the Spirit creates in us a new tension and a sense of want due to the perpetual gap between the fullness we receive in the present and that duly prepared for us in the future."[76] In Wesleyan terms, "One lives with a constant awareness of the unfinished character of salvation—an awareness that prevents any attainment of the goal from being falsely construed as arrival at the final destination."[77] Henry Knight says, "Each attainment along the way of salvation is actual in itself, but never a stopping point. Because the ultimate horizon is eschatological, there is no point in the Christian life where growth is no longer possible or desirable. There is always 'more.'"[78] Gordon Rupp defined this "more" as "new horizons of Christian experience."[79]

I think of this whenever I am an airline passenger arriving at a hub when the flight attendant announces, "If this is not your final destination . . ." No indeed, this is definitely not my final destination, even if this is where I am currently headed. Nothing and nowhere in this world or the next counts as a final destination, yet each in its own way may provide a partial fulfillment and a sign pointing beyond itself to someplace more,

---

73. Bence, "John Wesley's Teleological Hermeneutic," 33.

74. John Wesley, "Farther Thoughts on Christian Perfection," in Chilcote and Collins, *Works of John Wesley*, 13:110.

75. Palamas, *Gregory Palamas*, 18. Palamas says that the person experiencing sanctification "is being borne on to further progress and experiencing even more resplendent contemplation. He understands that his vision is infinite because it *is* a vision of the infinite, and because he does not see the limit of that brilliance; but, all the more, he sees how feeble is his capacity to receive the light" (39, italics his).

76. Matthew the Poor, *Communion of Love*, 184.

77. Bence, "John Wesley's Teleological Hermeneutic," 270.

78. Knight, *Anticipating Heaven Below*, 19.

79. Gordon Rupp, in Knight, *Anticipating Heaven Below*, 19.

closer to my destiny. This vision of limitless growth and discovery shows eternity to be endlessly fascinating.

John Wesley "plainly rejects the Roman Catholic doctrine of purgatory, arguing that 'no suffering but that of Christ has any power to expiate sin, and no fire, but that of love, can purify the soul either in time or eternity.'"[80] Yet Wesley envisions an infinite, eternal transformation. Within the context of Protestant-Catholic theological conflict in his day, Wesley "plainly rejects" a particular view of purgatory, not the possibility and necessity of further purification after death. It is entirely consistent with his theology of sanctification that the fire of God's love continues the unfinished process of perfecting each person, *even* after death. This is not to argue for an earned forgiveness, but simply to recognize the fact that even the most godly Christian will end this life without complete holiness. This is also consistent with Wesley's view of paradise on the way to the full experience of heaven.[81] Kenneth J. Collins offers a view that rejects Purgatory but affirms continued growth in heaven.[82]

The comprehensive transformation John Wesley envisioned for all of creation "is a *restoration* of the old order into its originally intended state, not the creation of a new universe *ex nihilo*."[83] This is a significant theme for Charles's hymns and preaching as well. "The Wesleyan hymns of the early 1740s were notable for their longing for sanctification,"[84] and again in one of his last hymns, Charles expressed his undying hope for sanctification and *theosis*: "Again I take the words to me / Prescribed, and offer them to Thee: / Thy kingdom come, to root out sin, / And perfect holiness bring in; / And swallow up my will in Thine, / And human change into divine."[85]

John Wesley believed very strongly in the grace-empowered transformation of God's people. "Conformed to God's image in a superlative translucent way, they shall radiate the divine glory throughout."[86] This vision is

---

80. John Wesley, in Bence, "John Wesley's Teleological Hermeneutic," 188; Colon-Emeric, *Wesley, Aquinas*, 154–57; Sangster, *Path to Perfection*, 65–70.

81. Bence, "John Wesley's Teleological Hermeneutic," 188–98. See Jerry Walls, *Purgatory*, and *Heaven, Hell, and Purgatory*.

82. Collins, *Theology of John Wesley*, 318–19. But see Payne, *Catherine of Genoa*, for a positive, transforming vision of a process which brings "the soul to its perfection" (79).

83. Bence, "John Wesley's Teleological Hermeneutic," 229, underscored in original.

84. Tyson, *Assist Me to Proclaim*, 238.

85. Ibid., 336.

86. Collins, *Theology of John Wesley*, 325.

clearly connected to the transfiguration and related Scriptures that speak of Christians experiencing and radiating God's glory.

Wesley's *Explanatory Notes on the New Testament* include reflections on the transfiguration in the Synoptic Gospels.

Regarding the version in Matthew: "His face shone with divine majesty, like the sun in its strength; and all his body was so irradiated by it, that His clothes could not conceal its glory, but became white and glittering as the very light with which He covered Himself as with a garment."[87]

Concerning Mark's description of Jesus' clothes as "shining, white as snow; such as no fuller can whiten" (Mark 9:3 KJV; NIV: "dazzling white, whiter than anyone in the world could bleach them"), Wesley added "Such as could not be equaled either by nature or art."[88]

Commenting on Luke's words "they saw his glory" (Luke 9:32 KJV/ NIV), Wesley noted that this was "the very same expression in which it is described by St. John (i.140), and by St. Peter (i:16)."[89] He also noted that when Moses and Elijah appeared "in glory," that glory was "like Christ with whom they talked," a particular example of the light enveloping all who enter the heavenly kingdom.[90]

Where the transfiguration appears in 2 Peter 1:16–18, Wesley describes Jesus as "shining from heaven above the brightness of the sun" and "a specimen of His glory at the last day."[91]

The implications of this become clearer as we look at Wesley's notes on closely related passages, such as 2 Peter 1:4 (KJV), "partakers of the divine nature," as "being renewed in the image of God, and having communion with Him, so as to dwell in God and God in you."[92] Concerning John 17:22, Wesley writes that "the glory of the only begotten shines in all the sons of God. How great is the majesty of Christians!"[93]

Clarence Bence explains, "because God created humanity with a capacity for the divine, Wesley can speak boldly of salvation in terms of participation in the divine nature, not by means of self-elevation, but by means

---

87. Wesley, *Explanatory Notes*, 84.

88. Ibid., 67.

89. Ibid., 235.

90. Ibid., 235.

91. Ibid., 893.

92. Ibid., 890.

93. Ibid., 376; Cf. Welsh Methodist Ann Griffith: " . . . to be on your holy mountain is high privilege indeed" (O'Malley, *Welsh Pilgrim's Manual*, 34).

of divine grace mediated to persons who appropriate the divine life through faith."[94] It is a process of restoration, of recovering God's original design for humanity, and its accomplishment comes only by sanctifying grace.[95]

Where Jesus says in John 17:24 (KJV), "that they may behold my glory, which thou hast given me," Wesley says, "Herein is the happiness of heaven" and points to 1 John 3:2.[96] In that passage, which says (KJV), "when he shall appear, we shall be like him; for we shall see him as he is," Wesley comments at some length:

> It is something ineffable, which will raise the children of God to be, in a manner, as God himself. *But we know*, in general, that *when he*, the Son of God, *shall appear, we shall be like him*—The glory of God penetrating our inmost substance. *For we shall see him as he* is—Manifestly, without a veil [referring to Moses]. And the sight will transform us into the same likeness.[97]

We also need to look at 2 Corinthians 3:18: "And we all, with unveiled face beholding as in a glass the glory of the Lord, are transformed into the same image from glory to glory, as by the Spirit of the Lord." (KJV) Here Wesley says, "We behold His glory in the glass of His word, and our faces shine too; yet we veil them not, but diffuse the lustre which is continually increasing, as we fix the eye of our mind more and more steadfastly on His glory displayed in the gospel."[98]

It is clear from John Wesley's brief notes that while he did not write at great length about the Transfiguration event, he saw the essence of its meaning and application to the transformation of the "children of God" (1 John 3:2 NIV). His comments on 2 Peter, 1 John, and 2 Corinthians especially describe what sanctification or theosis—our ultimate destiny—is all about. For Wesley, the way of salvation is "a process of redemption directed at nothing less than a complete transformation of sinful creatures into the very image of the Creator, while still retaining their full humanity."[99] Just as, for Orthodox theology, theosis is the ultimate purpose in life, for Wesley, "The goal of human existence is to be so united to God by faith that one

94. Bence, "John Wesley's Teleological Hermeneutic," 82.

95. Andreopoulos, *This Is My Beloved Son*, 60–61.

96. Wesley, *Explanatory Notes*, 377.

97. Ibid., 910 (italics his).

98. Ibid., 652.

99. Bence, "John Wesley's Teleological Hermeneutic," 3.

bears the very image of the divine and thus becomes a participant of the fullness of God."

John Wesley always maintained the possibility of "backsliding," a voluntary moving away from God at any stage of Christian life in this world.

> Thus, although man receives the grace of God and is made to participate in incorruptibility and deification through the communion of the sacraments, he runs the risk, throughout the duration of his earthly life, of falling away on account of his own sloth [or any form of sin].[100]

Wesley saw our transformation as a synergistic process, initiated by God but requiring our willing participation. "Participation in the divine nature extends beyond a spiritual relationship based upon forgiven guilt, to a cooperative activity with God in the renewal and restoration of the created order."[101] That synergy requires the possibility of refusal to cooperate at any stage in the process.

Wesley's vision makes room for instantaneous as well as gradual Christian perfection. His desire to avoid any idea of Purgatory creates a dilemma. Since "without holiness no one will see the Lord" (Heb 12:14 NIV), Wesley emphasizes "entire sanctification" in this life. Yet he also envisions an eternity of continued spiritual growth. All of this may have contributed to Wesley's reticence in writing about heaven. He does speculate on matters which flow from or are consistent with Scripture—including the presence of animals and the transformation of hostile natural forces, but on other matters he says little. Even so, Wesley's overall theology of hopeful transformation can enter into dialogue with Orthodox convictions about eternity. Perhaps because they think of salvation less juridically and view death, in terms of the sanctifying journey, with less finality, they can view the timetable of salvation with realism and balance. "Orthodox theologians are unanimous that our final deification will be realized only in the eschaton . . . nevertheless, a very sure and certain beginning should characterize all Christians in the present age."[102] Yet Orthodox, Wesleyans, and many others can agree that "Deification . . . is the ultimate purpose of God's creation."[103]

100. Mantzaridis, *Deification of Man*, 43.

101. Bence, "John Wesley's Teleological Hermeneutic," 129; see 123–30 on synergy in Wesley's theology.

102. Clendenin, *Eastern Orthodox Christianity*, 134, 135.

103. Ibid., 134–35.

The Wesleyan movement is part of the democratization of trans-formation. Reading the desert fathers could easily leave the impression that very few Christians are likely to respond to transforming grace with enough commitment and consistency to persevere on the way to heaven. As Sophrony Sakharov says, "Not many souls have the courage to step off the path trodden by the vast majority in this fallen world, to live according to Christ's commandments."[104] This is the import of Jesus' saying that "small is the gate and narrow the road that leads to life, and only a few find it" (Matt 7:14 NIV). Such is the result of free will, sinful distractions, and "the manifestations of pride" which "distort the divine image in man. Outside Christ, without Christ, there is no resolving the tragedy of the earthly his-tory of mankind."[105]

Yet in Christ "lies salvation for those who are united in His Name, and so for whole peoples, for the whole world [cf. John 4:42; Matt 12:21]. There is not, and cannot be, any situation in which He is powerless to save."[106] This realization on the part of the Wesleys and others echoes an assumption in 1 Peter 2:9 where Peter refers to *all* believers as "a chosen people, a royal priesthood, a holy nation, God's special possession, that you may declare the praises of him who called you out of darkness into his wonderful light" (NIV). So we read in 1 Timothy that "God our Savior . . . wants all people to be saved and to come to a knowledge of the truth" (1 Tim 2: 3–4 NIV). David Watson clearly expresses the Wesleyan view of salvation: "God wants every single person to receive the life-changing power of the Holy Spirit. God wants each of us to enter into the divine life of the Trinity, to know God and to be known by God."[107] So, as Henry Knight says, "the Wesleys took their message to all persons, believing all, not just a few, were eligible recipients of that salvation."[108]

In that hope and assurance, early Methodism carried the message of sanctifying grace and disciplined response to the masses. Wesley sought to make the goal and process of Christian perfection, as defined by love, accessible to all, attained not by "devotional or ascetic exercises," but by

104. Sakharov, *We Shall See Him*, 68.

105. Ibid., 30–31.

106. Ibid., 71; Cf. Russell, *Fellow Workers with God*, 169 and Lossky, *Mystical Theology*, 19.

107. Watson, *Scripture and the Life*, 125.

108. Knight, *Anticipating Heaven Below*, 18.

grace through faith.[109] Yet whether in a remote desert monastery or a Wesleyan class meeting, the priority of grace and the necessity of our response remains the same. "As God works in us, we work out our salvation, not by self-effort or by any inherent ability . . . but by the transforming grace of God that works in us to will and to do his will. (Phil 2:12–13)"[110] In fact, "Uncreated grace is so joined to our created nature that the two become one. And this is divinization."[111] It must also be said that while traditional monastic discipline would seem foreign to the Wesleyan movement, Wesley employed his own discipline, summarized in the General Rules and lived out in class meetings and other structures. There must inevitably be a way of life that encourages, motivates, and gives shape to our growth in grace.

Growth in grace opens heaven for God's people, beginning in this life. The Welsh Methodist poet Thomas Jones prayed:

> It is the manifestation of your glory which makes heaven what it is. This is the privilege of your children; by perceiving you here through faith they are beginning that perfect heaven, which they will enjoy perfectly when they have perfect vision of you.[112]

For this reason, "Heaven and earth are full of God's glory, shot through with the energies of his creative love."[113] There is no room for a spiritual individualism that seeks to live the transformed, transforming life apart from others or apart from the larger world. "The Gospel itself is eschatological in nature. In the same way that each individual is transformed and made holy as a new creature, so will all creation be transformed and made holy one day."[114]

Charles Wesley devoted considerable attention to personal and cosmic transformation—the destiny to which the transfiguration points and the Holt Spirit empowers. He sees transformed life "surrounded with the golden blaze, / Hid in the secret of his face."[115] He looks to the time when we "Transfigured shall with Christ appear, / With him in light and glory live."[116]

---

109. Bence, "John Wesley's Teleological Hermeneutic," 60.

110. Clendenin, *Eastern Orthodoxy*, 158.

111. Sakharov, *We Shall See Him*, 94.

112. Thomas Jones, in Allchin, *Praise*, 31.

113. Allchin, *Praise above All*, 78.

114. Pierce, *Enthroned on Our Praise*, 215.

115. Charles Wesley, in Kimbrough, *Partakers of the Life Divine*, 117.

116. Ibid., 115.

Charles's vision for the process of sanctification is "a progressive experience that lasts a lifetime" and which "does not take place in isolation, but rather within the life of community, the church—the body of Christ."[117]

Kimbrough points out that while Charles's references to the transfiguration are not as many or as systematic as the fathers or Gregory Palamas, the theme remains important and clearly linked to the process and goal of sanctification.[118] Wesley wrote of the day when those "Who Moses and the prophets hear, / And Christ the sum of all receive, / *Transfigured shall with Christ appear, / With him in light and glory live*."[119] Such a vision embodies both the boldness and humility with which he approached this great mystery. Wesley avoided any kind of detached spirituality regarding the transfiguration because he saw in it the connection Jesus himself made to suffering as well as to glory: "The image of the earthly now / The death we in our bodies bear, / And daily on his cross we bow, / The kingdom of our Lord to share; / The image of the heavenly Man, / Our bodies, spiritual as his / In that sabbatic day shall gain / with fullness of immortal bliss."[120]

For John and Charles Wesley, the hope embodied in the transfiguration was infinite and eternal. The possibilities for human transformation were endless, based always on the synergistic interplay of grace and faith, God's initiative and our grateful, willing response. The place the Wesleys hold in the Great Tradition connects explicitly with other strands in Christian teaching and practice, especially, though never exclusively, with those strands that are early and Eastern. They viewed the theology and experience of grace-empowered transformation in Christ to be the heart of their contribution and of the movement they launched. More than a doctrine to be explicated, theirs was a path to be walked with fellow pilgrims who shared their hope that humanity could be rescued from its "bent to sinning," and "changed from glory into glory."[121]

Out of this transforming vision came the explosive movement that attracted and mobilized vast numbers of Methodists in the great adventure of calling each other and the world to a life of holiness.

---

117. Kimbrough, *Partakers of the Life Divine*, 131, 132.

118. Ibid., 113, 120.

119. Ibid., 115; italics his.

120. Charles Wesley, in Kimbrough, *Partakers of the Life Divine*, 119.

121. Charles Wesley, "Love Divine, All Loves Excelling," *United Methodist Hymnal*, #384, vv. 2, 4.

# Chapter 6

# Participate in the Divine Nature? Necessary Disclaimers

Christianity has inherited from Israelite biblical theology a firm conviction that there is an ontological gap between the Creator and the creature.
—David Fagerberg, *Divinization*

We enter the eternal Kingdom, while preserving our personal being.
—Sophrony Sakharov, *We Shall See Him as He Is*

But the deification . . . that the Fathers had in mind does not mean the change of the human nature into a divine one. Rather, it means qualifying human nature for life with God in a communion of love.
—Matthew the Poor, *Orthodox Prayer Life*

The fact that God became a human being is a firm confirmation of our hope for the divine transformation of human nature. Humanity will be made divine just as God himself became a man. He who became man without any sin will deify human nature, yet without changing it into divine nature.
—Maximus the Confessor, *The Book of Mystical Chapters*

The Word renewed his image within humanity so that through it humanity can once more come to know God and be in his likeness.
—Lois Farag, *Balance of the Heart*

THERE IS IN THE West, especially among Protestants, a hesitancy, if not re-pugnance, when it comes to some of the language of transformation, even though much of that language is scriptural. Included among the causes for this concern are classical Greek, Roman, and Jewish philosophical, religious, and political concepts contributing to, yet are distinct from, early Christian theologies of transformation.[1] Also, some writers in the Western mystical tradition have prompted concern over the language and interpretation of mystical union.[2] Often the difficulty is over terminology.

One example is an article by Ben Drewery in which he argues against any kind of divinization language that seems to obliterate the distinction between Creator and creature. He is especially critical of any use of 2 Peter 1:4, believing that this letter is post-scriptural and reflective of Hellenistic philosophy. He rails against any identification with, or absorption into, the essence of God. I find this to be an overdrawn but necessary corrective to any careless presentation of *theosis* or transfiguration as somehow replacing our human nature with the nature of God.[3] While the identification of creature with Creator or the absorption of the creature into the Creator are not what is being put forward, given the word "*theosis*" and its translations, "deification" and "divinization," the concern is understandable and must be addressed.

Many, including Orthodox writers, issue disclaimers about this kind of misunderstanding, and while the language of *theosis* can seem provocative to Western ears, the intent is not to express any kind of divine-human identity, but rather a unity that is both communion and reflection. We are able to participate in the divine nature by at last having grace restore in us the image of God in which humanity was originally created. Thus we are invited to share God's character, but *always* and *only* as creatures: "the deified human person never stops being human." Finlan and Kharlamov make the point very clearly, saying, "Of course, Christian monotheism goes against any literal 'god making' of believers. Rather, the NT speaks of a transformation of mind, a metamorphosis of character, a redefinition of selfhood, and an imitation of God."[4] Frederica Mathewes-Green says that "even at the heights of *theosis*, your own personality remains intact, unified and made translucent, serving as a lantern for Christ's light."[5] As Ben

---

1. Collins, *Partaking in Divine Nature*, 2–3; 12–48; Cf. Finlan and Kharlamov, *Theosis*, vol. 1 and Kharlamov, *Theosis*, vol. 2.

2. Collins, *Partaking in Divine Nature*, 111–40.

3. Drewery, "Deification," 32–62, and criticism by Keating, *Deification and Grace*, 29.

4. Finlan and Kharlamov, *Theosis*, 6, 1.

5. Mathewes-Green, *Jesus Prayer*, 125.

Witherington puts it, "A close encounter with God . . . makes clear that God is God and we are not!"[6]

In a similar way, Theodore Runyan makes it clear that

> "Divinization" or "deification" (*theosis*) should not be understood as becoming a god, but . . . becoming what God created humanity to be, the image reflecting God as that creature whose spiritual senses are enabled to participate in, to be a partner, and to share in (*koinonia*) the divine life. However, the fact that "God hath been pleased to make the creature partaker in the Divine nature," says Macarius, does not in any sense erase the distinction between God and the human soul. If anything, this distinction is reinforced, preserved, and enhanced by the soul's being made a creaturely participant in divine energy. Were this a mystical merger, and absorption of the human soul into the divine, there would no longer be two, and therefore no longer an image or reflection of the divine in the human.[7]

Andrew Hofer also recognizes that "While the theme of divinization is essential to the Christian faith, some consider the language of divinization too dangerous or just flat out fundamentally wrong."[8] Yet he explains this "essential" teaching within his Catholic, but also scriptural and ecumenical, context, saying, "Catholics believe that salvation occurs through a real transformation that heals and elevates our nature to share in the divine nature."[9] We inherit eternal life as a gift, not as a right. We exhibit his truth and love, because his Spirit is purifying our hearts. We share his glory because we live in his presence. "Man is called to participate in God, without there being any confusion between his nature and that of God." And again, " . . . the union with God mentioned by the Fathers never amounts to a disintegration of the human person into the divine infinite, but, on the contrary, it is the fulfillment of his free and personal destiny."[10] Sophrony Sakharov makes it clear that "God, not man, is the Origin of Being; but man is created with the potential of receiving and eternally bearing within himself the non-created Life of Divinity."[11]

---

6. Witherington III, *We Have Seen His Glory*, 13.

7. Runyan, *New Creation*, 81.

8. Hofer, *Divinization*, 1.

9. Ibid., 3.

10. Meyendorff, *Christ in Eastern Christian Thought*, 126; 129.

11. Sakharov, *We Shall See Him*, 192.

Augustine taught that "even when we are like him and shall see him as he is (words which clearly imply an awareness of our present unlikeness), we shall still have no natural equality with him. For the created nature must always be less than the Creator."[12] In the same way, commenting on 1 John 3:2—"we shall be like him"—the Venerable Bede said "at the same time we shall be unlike him because he is our Creator and we are only creatures."[13] Edgardo Colon-Emeric notes that Thomas Aquinas, who accepted the language of *theosis*, "always protects the Creator-creature distinction."[14]

Protestants are accustomed to speaking of Christlikeness, and other expressions that point to divine transformation of life, character, and destiny. But Protestants and Western Christians generally hesitate and even recoil, as we have said, at some of the terms commonly used by Eastern Christians for essentially the same reality. Again, "For much of Western theology the concept of theosis creates unease and often hostile rejection as it appears to make humans into 'gods.'"[15] But Reformed theologian T. F. Torrance insists the "we share in the life of God while remaining what we are made to be, humans and not Gods." He further states:

> The staggering thing about this is that the exaltation of human nature into the life of God does not mean the disappearance of man or the swallowing up of human and creaturely being in the finite ocean of the divine being, but rather that human nature, remaining creaturely and human, is yet exalted in Christ in God's life and glory.[16]

Anthony Coniaris, a Greek Orthodox priest with a gift for communicating difficult or off-putting concepts, is very helpful when it comes to *theosis*: "Theosis is what God wants for us who are created in His own image: to become like Him in whose image we are made."[17] In terms reminiscent of the Wesleys and Adam Clarke, Coniaris says "Within each one of us God has placed the capacity for unlimited growth." *Theosis*, he says, "means becoming, becoming more and more like God in Christ as we go through life; becoming all that God wants us to become by His grace, growing to

---

12. Augustine, in Bray, *Ancient Christian Commentary on Scripture*, XI:195.

13. Bede, in Bray, *Ancient Christian Commentary on Scripture*, XI:195.

14. Colon-Emeric, *Wesley, Aquinas, and Christian Perfection*, 98.

15. Habets, "Reforming Theosis," in Finlan and Kharlamov, *Theosis*, 166.

16. T. F. Torrance, in Habets, "Reforming Theosis," in Finlan and Kharlamov, *Theosis*, 166–67.

17. Coniaris, *Tools for Theosis*, 21.

the fullest potential that God intends for us; becoming partakers of God's nature, gods by grace as Jesus is God by nature."[18]

We have seen that, for John Wesley, the panorama of grace which makes up the "great salvation," is "from the first dawning of grace in the soul till it is consummated in glory."[19] "The 'exchange formula'—God became human in order that humans may become divine—is very much a part of Charles Wesley's theology of participation."[20] Charles anchors this sanctifying vision in 2 Peter 1:4, a primary text for Orthodox writers.[21]

Since the use of *"theosis"* and its equivalents creates difficulties for many readers, it remains important to clarify what it is and what it is not. For Tuomo Mannermaa, for example, "When seen in the light of the doctrine of *theosis*, the Lutheran tradition is born anew and becomes once again interesting."[22] But he also finds in Luther that "this *unio* does not signify any change of substance. God does not stop being God, and man does not stop being man."[23] Baptist theologian Clark Pinnock says, "By the grace of God and *as creatures* we participate in [God] . . . without becoming God."[24] Mannermaa's view is that

> Divine life has manifested itself in Christ. In the church, understood as the body of Christ, human beings participate in this life and thereby partake of "the divine nature" (2 Pet. 1:4). This "nature," or divine life, permeates the being of humans like leaven permeates bread, in order to restore it to its original condition as *imago Dei* [image of God].[25]

Paul Collins and Robert Tuttle note that one source of uneasiness over *theosis* is a tendency for some Western writers to use "extravagant, and perhaps incautious language to describe the processes of becoming united with God" and "unguarded language of mystical union."[26] John

---

18. Coniaris, *Tools for Theosis*, 34, 64. Cf. Vickers, *Minding the Good Ground*, 89, on the connection between the various terms used for Spirit-driven transformation.

19. John Wesley, in Runyan, *New Creation*, 89.

20. Kimbrough, *Partakers of the Life Divine*, 138.

21. Ibid., 137.

22. Mannermaa, "Justification and Theosis," in Braaten and Jenson, *Union with Christ*, 25.

23. Mannermaa, "Fascinating," in Braaten and Jenson, *Union*, 11.

24. Clark Pinnock in Medley, "Participation," in Kharlamov, *Theosis*, 2:207.

25. Mannermaa, "Justification and Theosis," in Braaten and Jenson, *Union*, 26.

26. Collins, *Partaking in Divine Nature*, 137; Tuttle, *Mysticism in the Wesleyan*

Wesley, for example, was both fascinated and repelled by mystical writers. For Collins, "the distinction between the Creator and the creature . . . is often compromised, whether intentionally or otherwise" by the use of such "incautious language," which then "reinforces the views of those who find mystical theology in general and the metaphor of deification in particular repugnant."[27] Sophrony Sakharov says, "To speak of likeness to the point of identity troubled those who interpreted this as a complete fusion with God. There is, and always will be, an ontological distance between God, Who is unconditioned Primordial Being, and man, who is His creation."[28]

While participating in the divine nature (2 Pet 1:4) was central to Charles Wesley's theology, ministry, and writing, he avoided using language that would suggest such a merger of divine and human nature. "For Charles Wesley participation does not make of us something that we are not. It does not nullify our humanness."[29] Instead, we become "the persons God intends for us to be."[30] Charles's hesitation to use terms like "deification" is consistent with his critical appreciation for Christian mysticism and with his own Protestant sensibilities. He sought to keep his language scriptural, though his interpretation of Scripture was certainly through a patristic lens. Yet none of this should create the impression that his teaching concerning participation was at substantial variance with Eastern theologies of transformation in Christ.[31]

In his commentary on the Letters of Peter, Baptist theologian Douglas Harink explores the connection between the transfiguration and sharing in the divine nature, drawing extensively upon Orthodox theology. As we should expect, Harink distinguishes *theosis* or participation from any merged identity, and stresses the decisive role of grace, saying "Christians are made to share in Christ's divine sonship only through the grace and power of the life-giving Holy Spirit.[32] Similar disclaimers can be found across the centuries of Eastern thought, where the use of "*theosis*" and "deification" is common. Daniel Clendenin explains that,

---

*Tradition*, 25.

27. Collins, *Partaking in the Wesleyan Tradition*, 137.

28. Sakharov, *We Shall See Him,* 193.

29. Kimbrough, *Partakers of the Life Divine,* 145.

30. Ibid., 145–46.

31. Ibid., 141–43.

32. Harink, *1 and 2 Peter,* 145.

all the Eastern theologians, both ancient and modern, uniformly and categorically repudiate any hint of pantheism. Whatever it means to "become god," the essence of human nature is not lost. In this sense human theosis is a relative rather than an absolute transformation. There is a real and genuine union of the believer with God, but it is not a literal fusion or confusion in which the integrity of human nature is compromised. Orthodoxy consistently rejects the idea that humans participate in the essence or nature of God. Rather, we remain distinctly human by nature but participate in God by the divine energies or grace. At no point, even when deified, is our humanity diminished or destroyed.[33]

Thus we do well to hear the words of A Monk of the Eastern Church, who in his introduction to *Orthodox Spirituality* insists,

> there is no chasm between Eastern and Western Christianity. The fundamental principles of Christian spirituality are the same in the East and in the West; the methods are very often alike; the differences do not bear on the chief points. On the whole, there is one Christian spirituality with, here and there, some variations of stress and emphasis.[34]

The author specifically mentions John Wesley as someone the Eastern church "can acknowledge and honour" for "all that is so deeply Christian—and therefore 'Orthodox'" in his life and teaching. He shares the Orthodox insistence that "What is meant [by the term 'theosis'] is not, of course, a pantheistic identity, but a sharing, through grace, in the divine life . . ." He adds helpfully that "The incorporation of man into Christ and his union with God require the cooperation to two unequal, but equally necessary, forces: divine grace and human will," combining in active "synergy."[35]

It is always appropriate to remind ourselves and each other that

> theosis is a gift from God, it is not something we can obtain on our own. Of course, we must desire, struggle, and prepare ourselves so that we are worthy, capable, and receptive enough to accept and guard this great gift from God, since God does not wish to do anything to us without our freedom, but at the same time, Theosis is a gift of God.[36]

33. Clendenin, *Eastern Orthodox Christianity*, 130.
34. Monk of the Eastern Church, *Orthodox Spirituality*, x.
35. Monk of the Eastern Church, *Orthodox Spirituality*, xi; 22–23.
36. George, *Theosis*, 47.

*Theosis* is not an exotic option for some. "It is that which from the beginning has constituted the innermost longing of man's existence."[37] Transforming grace always requires and seeks our free and disciplined response.

Once we move away from contrasting terms to look at the reality they all seek to communicate, we find a common content, even if it takes different shapes within the cultural and ecclesiastical contexts in which it appears. That content is well expressed by Henry Scougal as

> a resemblance of the divine perfections, the image of the Almighty shining in the soul of man: nay, it is a real participation of his nature; it is a beam of the eternal light, a drop of that infinite ocean of goodness; and they who are endued with it may be said to have God dwelling in their souls and Christ formed within them.[38]

Pentecostal theologian Daniela Augustine notes that

> while the term [*theosis*] does not have a clear analogue in Protestant theology, the closest parallel to it would be John Wesley's idea of both the process of sanctification and the state of "entire sanctification". This parallel is not accidental since, as recent scholarship has established, Wesley's doctrine of sanctification was inspired by and developed in dialogue with the Eastern Church's understanding of *theosis*, as articulated in the writings of the Church Fathers.[39]

Paul Collins acknowledges that for much of their history, Western theologians have not used the terms "deification" or "*theosis*," yet important strands in Western theology are using the "architecture of the metaphor," even if they do not use the explicit language of "deification."[40] It is in our own time that ecumenical and multicultural cross-fertilization has allowed a broader appreciation for what is really an essential component of our common faith.

Stephen Finlan and Vladimir Kharlamov see the use of "transformation" as an equivalent for "*theosis*," (as I am doing,) "as an attempt to supplant patristic theology with standard Reformation language."[41] However, I believe "transformation" and its alternative, "transfiguration," can indeed convey the full meaning of "*theosis*" or "deification" once this usage is

---

37. Mantzaridis, *Deification of Man*, 12.

38. Scougal, *Life of God*, 34.

39. Augustine, "Liturgy, *Theosis*," in Martin, *Toward a Pentecostal Theology*, 169.

40. Collins, *Partaking in Divine Nature*, 112.

41. Finlan and Kharlamov, *Theosis*, 1:5.

clearly understood. While "*theosis*" may seem more precise, it also remains confusing—hence the careful explanations and disclaimers offered even by many Orthodox writers. Thus I continue to use the terms as equivalents, with "transformation" carrying the full significance of "*theosis*." In this way, I hope to speak to as wide a readership as possible by focusing on the heart of this experience, rather than nuances of language.

It is my conviction that spiritual transformation/sanctification/perfection/*theosis* is the purpose behind the incarnation, made visible in the transfiguration, and made possible by the cross and resurrection of Christ and the power of the Holy Spirit. Jason Vickers is right in saying that since this grace-empowered sanctification is essential to all we are and do as Christians, "what we ought to desire in our efforts to renew the church is nothing less than the sanctification and perfecting of the people of God."[42]

42. Vickers, *Minding the Good Ground*, 97.

# Chapter 7 ———————————————————————

# Transfiguration and Christian Unity

His face was like the sun shining in all its brilliance.
—*Rev 1:16 NIV*

O blessed communion, fellowship divine! We feebly struggle, they in glory shine; Yet all are one in thee, for all are thine. Alleluia, Alleluia!
— *"For All the Saints," The United Methodist Hymnal*

Unity without the divine presence is nothing more than an idea, a matter for discussion, or a vain longing. But in the presence of God unity becomes real and visible, overflowing and life giving, and many live it.
—Matthew the Poor, *The Communion of Love*

He bids us build each other up; / and gathered into one, / to our high calling's glorious hope / we hand in hand go on.
— *"All Praise to Our Redeeming Lord," The United Methodist Hymnal*

Communion with God and one another is the goal of the divinized life.
—Daniel A. Keating, *Divinization and Grace*

MANY THINGS BRING PEOPLE together, not all of them good. People often unite around a sport or hobby, a common vocation or cause. These can be helpful, or at least harmless, though they can also become obsessive or fanatical. People unite around ethnicity or political agendas, all too often to the point of hatred and violence. Sometimes a common enemy generates a kind of negative unity that divides one group or nation from another and opens the door to the twin curse of evil and death.

Two positive things that draw people together are a shared vision and a common destination, especially when they are rooted in God's love and empowered by grace. This is very different from using religion to increase the emotional horsepower behind an ungodly belief, campaign, or holy war. When God unites people in a common venture, the result is a blessing to everyone involved and to the world itself.

Traveling together is an amazing and underused way to build Christian community. I was once part of a pilgrimage to the Holy Island of Lindisfarne, in northeastern England. There were sixteen of us, all pastors and spouses. Everyone was ready for a break from everyday concerns and available for some in-depth spiritual refreshment.

As soon as our plane was in the air and even before, we began to break away. But our destination was even more important to the experience than our departure. We were going to one of those Celtic "thin places," where we actually expected to *be* and to *feel* closer to God. Each step on our journey—the airport at Edinburgh, the bus ride across the causeway, standing at last on the island itself, worshiping in the Church of St. Mary the Virgin—brought us closer to God and closer to each other.[1]

The common vision had been building for months, strengthened by communication with our on-site retreat leader, Barry Hutchinson, who would lead us on a prayer walk of the island. Barry also connected us with our morning speakers—David Adam, Kate Tristram, and Ray Simpson. We looked through photos of the island and read about its history. We were moved by the band Iona as they sang "Lindisfarne" and "Here I Stand." We celebrated Holy Communion, using a Celtic liturgy. In this sense our pilgrimage had already begun long before the plane left the ground. That common vision became our common destination as we drew closer to the island, and, at a deeper level, closer to God. Then the destination became our shared experience and indelible memory.

That kind of pilgrimage mirrors and strengthens the larger spiritual journey of life itself. Many common interests can bring people together in a limited way, but a spiritual journey connects us more deeply and permanently. In Christ, we are not only going with a few people to a place where God has been at work, but we are part of his body, headed *together* for his everlasting kingdom. There are no limits to this journey, or to the extent to which God may fill us with his transforming Spirit.

1. Cf. Dorotheos of Gaza, *Discourses and Sayings*, 138–39.

Spiritual growth and Christian community can also be built by traveling together on a mission trip and experiencing the mutual inspiration of working with people in another culture. People often begin a mission trip as a kind of one-way experience of "us helping them," but the reality is much different. Paul began a journey to Rome hoping to "impart some spiritual gift to make you strong," but he immediately restated his purpose, "that is, that you and I may be mutually encouraged by each other's faith" (Rom 1:11–12 NIV). John Wesley taught that serving others is a means of grace, a way of drawing closer to God through those we serve. Nearly everyone who returns from a mission trip talks about receiving more than they gave. That "more" is an expression of grace.

The transfiguration of Christ provides a clear and powerful image for our common vision and destiny as Christian disciples. That is why the transfiguration icon has such power to focus our lives and our prayers. The transfiguration, like a pilgrimage, lifts us up to Christ and opens us to his power for the often glorious, but also difficult, road ahead. Paul reminds us to turn our attention from lesser things and

> set your hearts on things above, where Christ is, seated at the right hand of God. Set your minds on things above, not on earthly things. For you died, and your life is now hidden with Christ in God. When Christ, who is your life, appears, then you also will appear with him in glory. (Col 3:1–4 NIV)

Too often we combine walking in isolation from our fellow travelers with a murky vision of where we're going. The result is that we focus too much on ourselves and the preoccupations of a given moment. Even when we celebrate joyful moments with family and friends, we can be disconnected with the source of our joy and its ultimate meaning. We need to lift our spiritual eyes up from the contours of the road immediately in front of us, and focus farther ahead on the Lord and where he is leading us.

Frequently this means asking the sometimes annoying "why questions." Whether we're working or reading or making an important decision, we need a clear connection between what we are doing and our purpose and direction in life. Everything we do should be consistent with our vision and destiny in Christ and moving us farther along "the path of life" he shows us (Ps 16:11 NIV).

As soon as we lose sight of our vision and our destination, our connection with God weakens and we disconnect from those who share our journey. As the clarity of our purpose dissipates, we can easily stumble and meander like those in Isaiah 59, who "look for light, but all is darkness; for brightness, but we walk in deep shadows. Like the blind we grope along a wall" (Isa 59:9–10 NIV). If we do this long enough, we become trapped in our immediate circumstances, or wander aimlessly until God helps us reconnect with himself, with his people, and with all that matters most in life.

Rick Warren's *The Purpose-Driven Life* addressed our need to be clear and focused about our God-given reason for existence—our purpose in life. He described the beauty and power of life when we live as the people God created and called us to be. Our grasp of God's purpose for our lives will only grow stronger as we glimpse the ultimate destiny God is planning for us. Jesus knew this so well when he assured his disciples that, in spite of the storm gathering around them, they could look beyond that storm to find hope:

> Do not let your hearts be troubled. You believe in God; believe also in me. My Father's house has many rooms; if it were not so, would I have told you that I am going there to prepare a place for you? And if I go and prepare a place for you, I will come back and take you to be with me that you also may be where I am. (John 14:1–3 NIV)

While at the time they could not understand what he was saying, Jesus' words were, like the transfiguration, pointing to a hopeful future, a future that was not an escape from struggle, suffering, or death, but one that would outlast them all. These words call for—in us, as they did in the disciples—faith and trust where our courage falters and our understanding fails. We can actually see this kind of faith in another setting: in Peter's response to Jesus' strange and off-putting words about his body and blood in John 6. When others began to shake their heads and wander off, "Jesus asked the twelve, 'Do you also wish to go away?' Simon Peter answered him, 'Lord, to whom can we go? You have the words of eternal life. We have come to believe and know that you are the Holy One of God.'" (John 6:67–69 NRSV)

Jesus' "words of eternal life," like his words about a house with "many rooms," point us beyond our limited selves and circumstances to remind us where this journey is going. They promise a destiny that remains within reach, by the grace of God. One of the better-known passages in the Letter to the Hebrews talks about the importance of this vision even to Jesus, who "for the joy set before him . . . endured the cross, scorning its shame, and sat down at the right hand of the throne of God" (Heb 12:2 NIV).

Hebrews reminds *us* of this to strengthen us to "run with perseverance the race marked out for us, fixing our eyes on Jesus, the pioneer and perfecter of faith" (Heb 12:1–2 NIV). Those who have lived by this hope have found in that hope the strength to carry it to others.

The transfiguration stands for all this and more. It opens our eyes and hearts to more of Jesus and more of our own destiny than we could ever "ask or imagine, according to his power that is at work within us" (Eph 3:20).

The passage just quoted from Ephesians goes on to lift up a beautiful doxology, whose meaning we may be only beginning to grasp: "to him be glory in the church and in Christ Jesus throughout all generations, for ever and ever! Amen" (Eph 3:21 NIV). In a way it is obvious that Christ should be praised and glorified "in the church . . . throughout all generations." But rather than leave it there, I want to suggest that every person in every generation, "for ever and ever!" needs to *see* something of Christ's glory, the glory the three disciples saw on the mountain, in order to receive that which is "immeasurably more than all we ask or imagine" (Eph 3:20 NIV).

The verses before this doxology speak of the content of the "immeasurably more," all of it part of the same closing prayer to this great letter. Paul seeks for his readers, and for us, "power through his [God's] Spirit in your inner being." He prays "that Christ may dwell in your hearts through faith," that we, "together with all the Lord's holy people," would be empowered "to grasp how wide and long and high and deep is the love of Christ," even though this love "surpasses knowledge." Then he goes farther! His prayer extends to a future that is both near and distant, immediate and infinite: "that you may be filled to the measure of all the fullness of God" (Eph 3:16–19 NIV). To be filled with the fullness of God is an astonishing, audacious hope, and it is not just that Paul is overcome with enthusiastic rhetoric as he wraps up his letter!

This is the same hope and prayer he has placed throughout Ephesians and Colossians. He sees in the body of Christ "the fullness of him who fills everything in every way." He describes God's people as "being built together to become a dwelling in which God lives by his Spirit." He calls us to build up the church in knowledge and service, to the point where we "become mature, attaining to the whole measure of the fullness of Christ" (Eph 1:23; 2:22; 4:13 NIV).

In Colossians, Paul prays that "God will fill you with all spiritual wisdom and understanding" so that "you may live a life worthy of the Lord and may please him in every way: bearing fruit in every good work, growing in the knowledge of God." All this and more, through God's power, is part of taking our place in "the kingdom of light." Paul sees the "mystery" of Christ in us as "the hope of glory," and works to "present everyone fully mature in Christ" (Col 1:9, 10, 12, 27, 28 NIV).

All of this reminds us of the connection between transformation, perfection, and Christian destiny. The path of life is not only heading for a far-off goal, but preparing us for that goal—fitting us for heaven, as the carol says.[2] We experience that preparation together as we walk toward our shared vision and common destiny, and as we "encourage each other and build each other up" along the way (I Thess 5:11 NIV). "By virtue of its nature and its aim, the Church constitutes a veritable 'communion of deification.'"[3]

Strong and loving Christian community, whether in a local congregation or among Christians across the planet, is a powerful witness to the reality of Christ in the world. The opposite is also true—the absence of love in the Christian community is a negative witness to Christ's reality in the world. Thus Jesus' prayer in John 17 that his followers would "be brought to complete unity. Then the world will know that you sent me and have loved them even as you have loved me" (John 17:23 NIV). Even with all its flaws, "the Church is appointed to lead her children into the sphere of Divine Being. She is the spiritual centre of our world, the focus of the whole history of mankind. . . . The Church is the bond of Christ's love by virtue of her indissoluble unity with Him."[4]

After two millennia of experience, we know how easily that unity is lost. Christians and their churches are and have been divided by everything from social class to ethnicity to conflicts over authority and doctrine. The "one holy catholic and apostolic church" we confess in the Nicene Creed has divided and subdivided into countless denominations and independent churches. Within congregations, we too often find conflict that repels newcomers, refuses resolution, and undermines mission. Among denominations and traditions, similar conflicts can last for centuries. As part of the Wesleyan tradition, I rejoice with Randy Maddox that Wesley's "integral connection of justification to this divinization bears promise for helping

---

2. Anon., "Away in a Manger," *United Methodist Hymnal*, #217, v. 3.

3. Gregory Palamas, in Mantzaridis, *Deification of Man*, 41.

4. Sakharov, *We Shall See Him*, 95–96.

to recover a theological wholeness that can contribute to the healing of the long-suffering divide between Eastern and Western Christianity."[5]

What can bring unity to the body of Christ when human nature is so good at this kind of divisiveness? There is a connection between glory and unity. The glory that is in Christ is the source of Christian unity and community. Jesus says he has already given us his glory—a probable reference to the transfiguration, along with the signs included in John's Gospel. But he also wants us to look ahead to the glory he will share with us in eternity: "Father, I want those you have given me to be with me where I am, and to see my glory, the glory you have given me because you loved me before the creation of the world" (John 17:24 NIV). This love, grounded in glory, "is a mystery which will only be fully revealed and realized in the age to come."[6] Yet it must begin here and now.

The more we see his glory, and live in the light of his glory, the more united we will be. The more we take our eyes off his glory and focus on ourselves, our situations, and each other, the more our human nature and the world around us will drive us apart. The light of the transfiguration transfigures *us*. Dorothy Lee notes that "The path of metamorphosis is not merely—or even primarily—a matter of individual conversion, but concerns the salvation of the whole community as the body of Christ."[7]

Just as Peter's second letter builds upon his experience of the transfiguration, John's first letter reflects his experience of Christ's glory. The glory which is a major theme in John's Gospel becomes a force that builds Christian community. Just as Jesus called to himself an unlikely collection of disciples, with himself as their source of unity, the Spirit continues to call together unlikely collections of disciples all over the world, unified by that same Jesus and by the Spirit Jesus sent. A significant part of that unifying dynamic is the glory these disciples have seen in Christ. Although John does not explicitly reference the transfiguration experience, the theme of glory is central to his message. "We have seen his glory," he says in the prologue to his Gospel, "the glory of the one and only Son, who came from the Father, full of grace and truth" (John 1:14 NIV).

On the basis of John's experience of Jesus' glory, which though unspoken included the transfiguration, and that of others who shared the same or other compelling experiences, he calls people into fellowship with himself

5. Maddox, *Responsible Grace*, 256.

6. Lossky, *Mystical Theology*, 232.

7. Lee, *Transfiguration*, 114.

and the entire body of Christian people. In 1 John, he immediately launches into this appeal:

> That which was from the beginning, which we have heard, which we have seen with our eyes, which we have looked at and our hands have touched—this we proclaim concerning the Word of life. The life appeared; we have seen it and testify to it, and we proclaim to you the eternal life, which was with the Father and has appeared to us. We proclaim to you what we have seen and heard, so that you also may have fellowship with us. And our fellowship is with the Father and with his Son, Jesus Christ." (1 John 1:1–3 NIV)

John's experience of Jesus' glory included signs, wisdom, sacrifice, and personal magnetism. Because he and other witnesses had "seen his glory," they could also share that glory, and in sharing it they found joy and community as disciples. "We write this," he says, "to make our joy complete" (1 John 1:4 NIV). Among those things "we have seen and heard" and shared with others was the realization that "God is light; in him there is no darkness at all" (1 John 1:5 NIV). Light joins glory as a major theme in John's Gospel and first letter.

In the fourth Gospel, Jesus reveals his glory in signs (John 2:11; 11:4, 40). His glory unites his followers as a vine is united to its branches, and in that unity bears fruit in the world (John 15:8). Glory is given and received between the Father and Son and shared with Jesus' disciples (John 17:1, 4–5, 22). Jesus is glorified through his disciples' faithfulness and prays that his disciples will see his glory through their fellowship with him (John 17:10, 24). Finally, as part of this great high priestly prayer, Jesus says "I have given them my glory that you gave me, that they may be one as we are one" (John 17:22 NIV). That unity in glory is not intended as a detached, mystical experience, but one that will demonstrate the reality of Jesus' mission in the world: "Then the world will know that you sent me and have loved them even as you have loved me" (John 17:23 NIV).

Both the Gospel and Letters of John stress the importance of love among Jesus' disciples in a way that parallels Peter's and Paul's concern for unity among believers (1 Pet 1:22; 3:8; Col 3:14). In John, that love is called "a new commandment" and through living out that commandment, the disciples will build credibility as Christ's ambassadors in the world (John 13:34–35 NIV). First John encourages Christians to follow this new commandment, "the message you heard from the beginning: We should love one another" (3:11 NIV). He explains the depth and seriousness of that love, saying "This is how we know what love is: Jesus Christ laid down his life for us. And we ought to lay down our lives for our brothers and sisters" (1 John 3:16 NIV). He lists practical ways to love "not . . . with words or speech but with actions and in truth" (1 John 3:18 NIV). He speaks of the divine origin of love, saying "let us love one another, for love comes from God" (1 John 4:7 NIV). That love from God is the reason and inspiration for Christian love—"We love because he first loved us," (1 John 4:19) and John warns that failure to love people turns any claim to love God into a lie.[8]

In other words, a life lived in glory produces unity defined by love. As we walk the path of life together, the people in our lives become means of grace for the journey, rather than distractions to avoid or hurdles to jump. In the light and glory of Christ, marriage, family, friendship, and Christian community all serve to sanctify our days and bring us closer to God. The witness of the church in every land and throughout all time can serve to strengthen and teach us in ways we could never manage in debilitating isolation. In spite of the many failures of Christians and churches to live up to the new and great commandment, we can also testify to the countless times that commandment has produced blessings in our lives and in the world.

My own life has been immeasurably enriched by meeting and reading Christians from amazingly varied traditions and cultures, both nearby and far away. I think of Christian friends living in persecution, monasteries that lift all of us up in prayer, communities like Walk to Emmaus, churches ranging from Amish to Coptic Orthodox, and Christians with very different personalities and interests. I give thanks for my own Wesleyan tradition, whose founders could see, beyond the divisions of their own time, the One who gives life to us all. "The result of this sharing in Christ is that believers participate in heavenly realities." Those "heavenly realities" bind us together in hope as "life takes on a heavenly dimension."[9]

This is the deep and rich fellowship that will "make our joy complete" (1 John 1:4). When we shine with the light of Christ, sharing a common vision of his glory and walking together as pilgrims toward his destiny, then the one holy catholic and apostolic church comes together in us. Therefore,

8. First John 4:20–21; Cf. Paul's descriptions of love and unity in the body of Christ in Romans 12, 1 Corinthians 12 and 13, and Ephesians 4:1–5.

9. Boersma, *Heavenly Participation*, 4–5.

as St. Benedict said, "Let [us] prefer nothing whatever to Christ, and may he bring us all together to everlasting life."[10]

Our unity here in this life both prefigures and reflects the apocalyptic vision in which "a great multitude that no one could count, from every nation, tribe, people and language" worships the One who is the source of our unity (Rev 7:9 NIV). Thus, for Charles Wesley, "the glory of heaven . . . is a shared glory."[11] There,

> we will see each other in that place where shall be gathered all the nations that have lived from the beginning of the world and to its very end. O God, grant that we may see each other there, where God is seen face to face, and gives new life to those who see Him, and comforts and gladdens them, and gives ineffable joy for all eternity. There men shine like the sun; there is true life; there is true honor and glory; there is true joy and gladness; there is true ecstasy, and all that is eternal and endless.[12]

Fellow pilgrims encourage one another as part of the communion of saints, along with the "great cloud of witnesses" of other times and places who also encourage us (Heb 12:1 NIV).

Norman Russell summarizes the necessary connection between transformation and unity: "Deification is a state of profound communion with God and with each other. Although consummated in the kingdom of heaven, it begins in the worshiping community."[13] It is in the experience of this "worshiping community" that we see the depths of this connection. We see it in the earliest gatherings in Acts, where communion among believers is—along with prayer, Word and Eucharist—an essential component of worship (Acts 2:42), and we see it in this prayer from the ancient Liturgy of St. James: "lead all to perfection, and make us perfectly worthy of the grace of Your sanctification, gathering us together within Your holy Church."[14]

The universal church and each worshiping community are, or should be, traveling on a kingdom pilgrimage that unites all participants in boundless hope. This common purpose and direction are the bases and inspiration for life and worship that is genuinely Christian. It is a journey which transcends and ultimately supersedes anything else Christians and their

10. Fry, *Rule of St. Benedict*, 73:11–12; p. 295.

11. Stevick, *Altar's Fire*, 139.

12. St. Tikhon of Zadonsk, in Manley, *Bible and the Holy Fathers*, 41.

13. Russell, *Fellow Workers with God*, 41.

14. Humphrey, *Grand Entrance*, 82.

churches may do along the way. In the words of a traditional gospel song, "This train is bound for glory."

# Chapter 8

# Transfiguration and Worship

Christian communal worship is the glorification of God and the sanctification of humanity as a divine-human event where God offers transformation and healing to help people become more fully what God created them to be and do.
—Brent D. Peterson, *Created to Worship*

Sanctify our souls, our minds and our bodies and grant that we may serve you in holiness all the days of our lives.
—Roberta Ervine, *Worship Traditions in Armenia and the Neighboring Christian East*

What matters is that in worship we should enter the presence of the living God.
—N. T. Wright, *For All God's Worth*

All at once we're ushered into heaven / To taste and see
—"Once for All," Mark Swayze and Denise Webb

Let my union with Thee, today, be forever, for through it, I increase and grow firm in virtue, wax strong in faith, and my hope becomes strong.
—*Agpeya*, Prayer after Communion

THOUGH MUCH HAS BEEN said about the purpose of worship, there now seems to be a kind of united voice coming from a wide spectrum of traditions. One of them is contemporary worship leader Bob Kauflin, who says that "God intends to transform us into his image as we behold his glory."[1] The connection between transfiguration and worship could not be clearer!

1. Kauflin, *Worship Matters*, 150.

James Payton, who has long been involved in Protestant-Orthodox conversations, writes that "As the church meets to worship God, we enter into his presence and experience communion with him. We were created to seek this communion and be drawn by it to his likeness, so worship furthers our divinization."[2] Lee Roy Martin says "the ultimate purpose and goal of worship is to transform the worshiper into the image of God. The more we worship, the more we become like God."[3]

Pentecostal scholar R. H. Gause connects the transfiguration to the experience of worshipping Christians, beginning with the early church, which "needed an experience of the future apocalyptic kingdom. This experience is provided in the narrative of the Transfiguration." In worship, "the repetition of stories [such as the transfiguration] provided the community with a means to re-experience what was recorded or to pre-experience what was promised." Through hearing the scriptural account of this amazing event, "believers experienced the glory of the kingdom in consummation." Indeed, "the Transfiguration account provided an effective instrument for the proleptic [anticipatory] realization of the kingdom of God." By the power of the Spirit, they were "translated 'in the Spirit' into the age to come." In other words, for Gause, far from being simply a story to be remembered and wondered at, "The narrative of the Transfiguration kept before the worshipping community the consciousness of what the kingdom of God was to be like. By this story, they were drawn into it and experienced it."[4] Congregations were transformed by the vision and power of what they "saw" as they accompanied Peter, James, and John, so to speak, up "the sacred mountain" (2 Pet 1:18 NIV).

Dorothy Lee has said that "The Transfiguration needs to be restored to its rightful place at the heart of Christian theology, if we are to regain its beauty in the life and worship of the Church."[5] Worship is incomplete if it remains earthbound, or focused entirely on the present. When we worship God, we should expect—without presumption, but with trust—that God will be there in transforming power.

We need to find in worship a transfiguring vision that draws us forward in hope. As A. M. Allchin put it, "Our eyes need to be cleansed by a light from beyond this world before they can see clearly what it is that lies

2. Payton, *Light from the Christian East*, 15.

3. Martin, *Toward a Pentecostal Theology*, 64–65.

4. Gause, "Lukan Transfiguration Account," 224; 219, 222, 223, 225, 237; Cf. 133.

5. Lee, *Transfiguration*, 137.

before us."[6] In worship, as in all of life, "The new creation . . . is for those who live out of the future and not primarily out of the past."[7] In worship, as on the holy mountain, God provides "a foretaste of the future kingdom."[8] In the words of Matthew the Poor, "Union with God is the aim of the life of prayer and worship. It is a foretaste of the glory Christians will enjoy in the age to come."[9] A prayer in the Coptic Liturgy compares the transforming experience of Communion, where "our souls will change to share your glory and our souls will unite with Your divinity," to that of the disciples on the mountain of transfiguration.[10] Another writer makes the same comparison, calling the Eucharistic prayer "the miracle of the transfiguration," in which "*the grace of our Lord Jesus Christ* 'takes' us out of the world in which we live and 'leads us up' . . . the high mountain of the love of God the Father." For in Holy Communion, our "hearts are on high, where Jesus Christ is, seated at the right hand of God (Col. 3:1)."[11]

Worship, like the transfiguration, takes place on a kind of mountain, yet in the midst of the full range of human experience. Luke says "Jesus took Peter, James and John with him and led them up a high mountain," no doubt recalling other mountains, from Sinai to the hill above Capernaum.[12] Like the temple and our own places of worship, a mountain could be the meeting place between God and his people. Both mountains and sanctuaries have brought me into God's presence in unforgettable ways. I think of Mount Saviour Monastery, near Elmira, New York, where I have made retreats for some fifty years. There are the monasteries of Meteora in Greece, Gallarus Oratory in the western mountains of Ireland, and St. Mary's Church on Lindisfarne. The reader will have another list. The memory of each one reminds us of an encounter with God that transformed us in some way. Each was "a foretaste of the future kingdom."

That foretaste comes to us in many ways as we worship. Included in these means of grace are Scripture and prayer. Norman Russell says "The Scriptures are sanctifying and deifying for through them God conforms human beings to his own likeness." Indeed, "Through the Scriptures Christ's

6. Allchin, *God's Presence Makes the World*, 87.

7. Witherington, *Rest of Life*, 8.

8. St. Jerome, in McGuckin, *Transfiguration of Christ in Scripture*, 273.

9. Matthew the Poor, *Orthodox Prayer Life*, 112.

10. *Coptic Liturgy*, 250.

11. Gregorios, *Divine Liturgy*, 220; 222, italics his.

12. Luke 9:2 NIV; Cf. Ratzinger, *Eschatology*, 309, 314.

teaching is implanted in our hearts, assimilating us to God and making us divine."[13] All of this is part of "the *epektasis*, the never-ending progress in to the mysteries of the spiritual life."[14]

Henry Scougal noted that "in prayer we make the nearest approaches to God and lie open to the influence of heaven. Then it is that the sun of righteousness doth visit us with his directest rays, and dissipateth our darkness, and imprints his image on our souls."[15] This is surely true of genuine, corporate worship, as it is with prayer in general. Worship puts us in touch with the transforming reality of the Maker and Restorer of the universe. Edith Humphrey says that in Old Testament worship, "the boundary between heaven and earth" is "startlingly permeable."[16] And so it is whenever we come together to worship in God's holy and transforming presence.

Within worship, Holy Communion in particular is a place of divine encounter and a means of grace for the sanctifying journey. Lorna Khoo, Daniel Stevick, and others describe Wesley's as a Eucharistic revival.[17] Khoo describes the impact of masses of Wesley converts descending upon unprepared Anglican parishes in search of the Sacrament. "Holy Communion to the Wesleys was a dynamic encounter which could be experienced and which changed lives."[18] Geoffrey Wainwright speaks of "the sacramental revival that for the Wesley brothers was integral to the growth and spread of real religion or vital Christianity."[19] S. T. Kimbrough says that John and Charles Wesley "pioneered a return to the Eucharistic ecclesiology of the ancient church," and Wainwright demonstrates the theology of early Christian worship (often mediated through the Anglican tradition) in Wesleyan Eucharistic hymns.[20] Their attempt, expressed in John's sermon "The Duty of Constant Communion," was to restore the Eucharist to the place it had in early Christian worship.[21]

---

13. Russell, *Doctrine of Deification*, 125; Cf. 127.

14. Ibid., 244.

15. Scougal, *Life of God*, 92.

16. Humphrey, *Grand Entrance*, 75.

17. Khoo, *Wesleyan Eucharistic Spirituality*, xvi; Stevick, *Altar's Fire*, 4–6.

18. Khoo, *Wesleyan Eucharistic Spirituality*, 62.

19. Wainwright, "'Our Elder Brethren Join,'" 6.

20. Kimbrough, *Partakers of the Life Divine*, 78; Wainwright, "'Our Elder Brethren Join.'" Cf. Rattenbury, *Eucharistic Hymns of John*.

21. Outler, *Works of John Wesley*. 3:427–39; Cf. Stevick, *Altar's Fire*, 25.

For Charles, the Eucharist was a central means of transforming grace for individuals and for the church.[22] His eucharistic hymns portray Holy Communion as a sanctifying, unifying mystery for God's people. "We may not understand how we become one as the body of Christ and with Christ in the Eucharist, but we can experience the mystery and the reality."[23] Wesley wrote in one of his hymns:

> O the depth of Love Divine, / the unfathomable grace! /
> Who shall say how bread and wine / God into us conveys? /
> How the bread his flesh imparts, / How the wine transmits his blood, /
> Fills his faithful people's hearts / with all the life of God!"[24]

The Wesleys saw worship, and the sacraments in particular, as a way in which God conveys transforming grace to the human heart. "The sacraments as *means* of grace particularly emphasize [John] Wesley's continuity between the divine and human realms. Baptism and Holy Communion . . . are vehicles of present attainment of salvation and a token of God's continual grace upon the life of the believer."[25] Hal Knight describes the deep and far-flung impact of this grace in our lives and in the world:

> The God who in the end will make all things new is even now, through the Spirit, transforming the hearts and lives of persons in love, manifesting the divine presence in worship and life together, and then enlisting them in a present work of renewing both church and society. Even now, God is bringing heaven below.[26]

The connection between transfiguration and Holy Communion may at first seem strange or far-fetched, but within the larger realities of grace and worship, it is well attested and makes sense. The Eucharist is the repeated, normal means of encountering the kingdom that was revealed on the mountain, "the liturgical experience of the transfiguration of the entire church in Christ."[27] Holy Communion is a means for God's transforming work within us. It is bread for the journey toward our destiny in Christ, a sign and experience of hope. Following John Wesley, "we can understand

22. Kimbrough, *Partakers of the Life Divine*, 76–78.

23. Kimbrough, *Partakers of the Life Divine*, 85.

24. Charles Wesley, "O the Depth of Love Divine," *United Methodist Hymnal* #627, v. 1.

25. Bence, "John Wesley's Teleological Hermeneutic," 274, italics his.

26. Knight, *Anticipating Heaven Below*, 13.

27. Andreopoulos, *This Is My Beloved Son*, 86–87.

Holy Communion 'refreshing our souls . . . with the hope of glory.'"[28] Far from being an empty ritua, "What the Eucharist invites us to experience is a new form of life where the old ways of the world are replaced by a new community of holy love."[29] Rob Staples has rightly described Holy Communion as "the sacrament of sanctification and thus ties sacramental spirituality with Wesley's doctrine of Christian perfection."[30]

The Eucharist is a kind of unequal gift exchange—"I bring to the chalice all I can, my entire being . . . and I receive in return the entire life of Christ."[31] "The entire life of Christ" in Communion offers "the transfiguration of the human condition," as we enter "the kingdom of God, albeit in a partial way, a symbolic and liturgical way."[32] For Daniel Brevint, "Here we are in a special Manner invited to offer up to God our Souls, our Bodies, and whatever we can *give*: And God offers to us the Body and Blood of his Son, and all the other Blessings which we have Need to *receive*."[33]

For John and Charles Wesley, the Eucharist is, in the words of Daniel Brevint, "not a representation only, but a means of grace."[34] God's sanctifying presence is the heart of the experience of the Lord's Supper, where we anticipate the time when "earth is turned to heaven." Hence, "We come with confidence to find / Thy special presence here," where "The fulness of our God made man / We here with Christ receive." The ancient *epiclesis* or invocation of the Holy Spirit appears in one of the *Hymns on the Lord's Supper*, which prays, "Come, Holy Ghost, / Thine influence shed, / And realize the sign; / Thy life infuse into the bread, / Thy power into the wine."[35] Jason Vickers has elaborated on this theme in describing the power available in the Eucharist through the outpouring of the Holy Spirit:

> According to the testimony of the saints, the Holy Spirit is present
> and at work through the sacramental life of the church, restoring
> us to the image of God; enabling us to know and love God with

28. Wesley, "Duty of Constant Communion," in Thompson, *Means of Grace*, 68.

29. Thompson, *Means of Grace*, 70.

30. Rob Staples, in Leclerc, *Discovering Christian Holiness*, 129.

31. Fr. Zacharias, in Andreopoulos, *This Is My Beloved Son*, 32.

32. Andreopoulos, *This Is My Beloved Son*, 111; 87.

33. Brevint, "Preface," in Wesley and Wesley, *Hymns on the Lord's Supper*, 3, caps and italics his; Cf. Stevick, *Altar's Fire*, 21–25 on Brevint's importance for the Wesleys' sacramental theology.

34. Wainwright, "'Our Elder Brethren Join,'" 16.

35. Charles Wesley, in Wainwright, "'Our Elder Brethren Join,'" 20, 24, 27.

all our heart, mind, soul, and strength; helping us to know how rightly to love our friends and even our enemies; reconciling us to God the Father through Jesus Christ, the eternally begotten Son; empowering us for worship and witness, and so on. . . . Through the sacramental life of the church, God redeems, transforms, heals, and sanctifies us. In and through the sacramental life of the church, God fills us with the presence and power of the Holy Spirit and with all grace."[36]

Jason Vickers's emphasis on transformation toward heaven resembles another one more than a thousand years earlier, part of a medieval eucharistic liturgy quoted by Tomas O'Sullivan:

In the holy mystery of this table we prepare for the kingdom of heaven, that is, in taking up the body and blood of our Lord Jesus Christ, coming from heaven through the Holy Spirit (who is the pledge of our inheritance); until we may come to that inheritance and will be like him.[37]

Thomas à Kempis said of the capacity of Holy Communion to transform, "In this sacrament grace is granted, the soul's lost strength is restored, and its beauty, often disfigured by sin, returns again." Indeed, the Eucharist can enable us to "share in eternal glory"[38] In this he agrees with Ignatius of Antioch that Communion is "the medicine of immortality," not in any magical way, but by serving as a God-appointed conduit of transforming grace.[39] Henry Knight says, "Through the Holy Spirit the faithful participant in the Lord's Supper receives both heaven in the heart, and experiences heaven yet to come, both foretastes of the full renewal of creation."[40] Thus Charles Wesley says that in that Supper, "He gives our souls a taste, Heaven into our hearts he pours"[41] For Wesley, "The supper brings heaven near, and it transports the communicants to heaven itself."[42] Sacramentally and eschatologically, "its end and completion is the Church's entrance into heaven, her fulfilment at the table of Christ, in his kingdom."[43] Geoffrey

36. Vickers, *Minding the Good Ground*, 76.

37. O'Sullivan, in Ryan and Leahy, *Treasure of Irish Christianity*, 267.

38. à Kempis, *Imitation of Christ*, 167, 170.

39. Ignatius, "Letter of Ignatius," in Richardson, *Early Christian Fathers*, 93.

40. Knight, *Anticipating Heaven Below*, 35–36.

41. Charles Wesley, in Knight, *Anticipating Heaven Below*, 35.

42. Stevick, *Altar's Fire*, 138.

43. Schmemann, *Eucharist*, 27.

Wainwright points out how distinctive (in the West) was the Wesleys' future eschatological orientation in *Hymns of the Lord's Supper*, including Eucharist as participation in and preparation for heaven and the heavenly banquet.[44]

Remembering has always held an important place in the theology and experience of Holy Communion, with echoes of Israel's Passover celebrations and Jesus' own instruction to "do this in remembrance of me" (1 Cor 11:24 NIV). For some Protestant traditions, remembrance is the central purpose of the Lord's Supper, but for all traditions the eucharistic words and actions recall that great moment in the Upper Room and the sacrifice it represents.

For other churches, however, including my own Wesleyan tradition, remembering expands to include the transforming presence of Christ in the Sacrament, though precise explanations of that presence vary. As Brent Peterson puts it, "memory does not fixate on Calvary but instead on a present encounter of the Last Supper that both illumines and inaugurates the kingdom of God aimed at a cosmic theosis, the renewal of all things into the Triune Godhead." Peterson sees this "theotic encounter" as transforming and motivational for the body of Christ as it seeks to live its discipleship in an often hostile world.[45] Peterson joins his own Wesleyan perspective to that of prominent Orthodox writer John Zizioulas, who describes the eucharistic liturgy as "an icon of the kingdom."[46] Sarah Heaner Lancaster expresses the connection between the Eucharist and transformation in the Wesleys, saying "Although John and Charles held somewhat different understandings of perfection, the Eucharist served a common purpose of empowering us to receive the fullness of God's saving work in this life."[47]

Pope Benedict XVI makes very clear the connection between the Eucharist and Christian unity:

> As Saint Paul says, "Because there is one bread, we who are many are one body, for we all partake of the one bread." (*I Cor 10:17*) Union with Christ is also union with all those to whom he gives himself. I cannot possess Christ just for myself; I can belong to

44. Wainwright, *Eucharist and Eschatology*, 72–74; 92–93, 139.

45. Brent Peterson, "Eschatology and Eucharist," in Vickers, *Wesleyan Theology of the Eucharist*, 102.

46. Brent Peterson, in Vickers, *Wesleyan Theology of the Eucharist*, 107.

47. Sarah Heaner Lancaster, "Soteriology and Eucharist," in Vickers, *Wesleyan Theology of the Eucharist*, 99.

him only in union with all those who have become, or will become, his own. Communion draws me out of myself towards unity
with all Christians.[48]

This connection is reflected also in Communion prayers of the *Didache*, an early manual of church teaching and practice:

> As this piece [of bread] was scattered over the hills and then was
> brought together and made one, so let your Church be brought
> together from the ends of the earth into your Kingdom. . . . Re-
> member, Lord, your Church, to save it from all evil and make it
> perfect by your love. Make it holy, "and gather" it "together from
> the four winds" into your Kingdom which you have made ready
> for it.[49]

Lawrence Farley says of the connection between the Eucharist and
transfiguration,

> Having received His holy and life-creating Mysteries, we do not
> instantly return to the same mediocre life we knew before. Instead,
> having been inwardly transfigured, we long to remain with our
> Lord for as long as possible, meditating on His righteousness,
> singing of His glory. Like the apostles on the Mount of Transfigu-
> ration, we cry out, "Lord, it is good to be here!" (Matt. 17:4). We
> have basked in His light and are reluctant to leave.[50]

For Georgios Mantzaridis, "Through Holy Communion, Christ enters
into the depths of man's existence with the offer of his divinizing grace."[51]
The transformational perspective lives also in Charles Wesley, who "un-
equivocally shares the Orthodox view that through the sacrament of Holy
Communion one is deified and God's nature is made known." So important
was this connection that Charles encouraged *daily* Communion and saw
Communion as essential to Christian worship—"the end and design of
Christians meeting together."[52] "Thus," says Kimbrough, "to refuse partici-
pation in the Eucharist is to refuse participation in the divine life and the
Spirit."[53] While Charles, like his brother, showed caution regarding mysti-

48. Benedict XVI, *God is Love*, 17–18.
49. Didache, in Richardson, *Early Christian Fathers*, 175–76.
50. Farley, *Let Us Attend*, 92.
51. Mantzaridis, *Deification of Man*, 55.
52. Kimbrough, *Partakers of the Life Divine*, 51, 53.
53. Ibid., 54.

cism, he did not hesitate to articulate, fully and often, a Eucharistic theology of "participation in the divine nature." Indeed, it is the main thrust of his approach to understanding the Sacrament. Long before, Paul prayed that his readers might "be filled to the measure of all the fullness of God" (Eph 3:19 NIV). For Wesley, one way this could happen was and is participation in the Eucharist:

> Now, Lord, on us Thy flesh bestow,
> And let us drink Thy blood,
> Till all our souls are fill'd below
> With all the life of God.[54]

But the transfiguring impact of Holy Communion is not confined to the liturgy only. The Wesleys emphasized that "Through the power of the Holy Spirit, the life of the coming kingdom is already breaking into the present, beginning in human hearts, and spreading from there to families, communities, and nations."[55] While freely acknowledging mystery as to the precise way God uses the sacraments to divinize, Charles Wesley believed that God "mystically links human and divine natures through the elements of bread and wine."[56] In this linking of natures within the eucharistic experience, "God glorifies us so that we may bring others to that experience of glory as well."[57] To this end, "Divinization is becoming icons of Christ through the liturgy." As "icons," transformed Christians shine the light of Christ into the world, so that "God . . . accompanies them out into the world he so loves, to make it, too, the dwelling place of God."[58] Thus, "We must see the world now in light of Mt. Tabor streaming from the liturgy out the stained glass windows to color our everyday life."[59] There is nothing narrowly individualistic in God's life-saving, transforming mission. Sanctification applies the full message and purpose of the Gospel to the full extent of human need. "Christ is still the content; eternal life is still the end; and the scope is still all humanity, lest they walk any longer in the shadow

---

54. Charles Wesley, in Rattenbury, *Eucharistic Hymns*, H-11.

55. Knight, *Anticipating Heaven Below*, xiii.

56. Kimbrough, *Partakers of the Life Divine*, 60.

57. Farley, *Let Us Attend*, 95.

58. Hofer, *Divinization*, 11, 13.

59. David Fagerberg, in Hofer, *Divinization*, 29.

of death without hope."[60] For this reason, we can never be "satisfied with solutions beneath the level of divinization."[61]

Holy Communion also reaches into the future "as a foretaste of the heavenly banquet."[62] Participation is far more than a merely present experience augmented by a dramatic representation of the Last Supper. The Eucharist anticipates and even participates in future reality. "Until it finds fulfillment in the kingdom of God," the Lord's Supper serves as "a *Pledge* from the Lord that he will give us that glory."[63] The Eucharist, as a present means of grace, empowers the transformation that flows from and leads toward eternal life. "As Christ promised, in that day, we will shine like the sun in the Kingdom of our Father" (Matt 13:43). In the Divine Liturgy, we even now take our weekly journey to that Kingdom."[64] The Spirit "raises us up to the heavenly sanctuary, the throne of God."[65] In worship, our hearts and our vision of reality expand not only within ourselves and toward God, but beyond ourselves. The movement inward and outward defines the transfiguring capacity of worship:

> The transfiguration . . . provides a pattern for us, a paradigm of prayer worth emulating in our own lives. The pattern essentially presents contemplation and action. It points us to an understanding of worship that incorporates both catching a glimpse of the divine and translating that vision into action in the life of the world.[66]

On the Holy Island of Lindisfarne, this picture of empowerment and engagement is often celebrated in reflections on the inward and outward flow of tides. Lindisfarne is a tidal island, connected to the English mainland at low tide, accessible by a modern road, but at high tide it is cut off altogether until the road appears from beneath the North Sea once again. The rhythm of the tides invites engagement and retreat; time to carry the presence of Christ into the world and time to "Come with me by yourselves to a quiet place and get some rest" (Mark 6:31 NIV). All of this is part of,

60. David Fagerberg, in Hofer, *Divinization*, 30.

61. Benedict XVI, quoted by David Fagerberg, in Hofer, *Divinization*, 26.

62. Lee, *Transfiguration*, 136.

63. Luke 22:18 NIV; Brevint, "Preface," in Wesley and Wesley, *Hymns on the Lord's Supper*, 17, italics his.

64. Farley, *Let Us Attend*, 96.

65. Schmemann, *Eucharist*, 37.

66. Chilcote, *Changed from Glory into Glory*, 20.

and flows from, being in God's presence in worship.[67] The fruit is character that is transformed and transforming.

> Union with God is the aim of the life of prayer and worship. It is a foretaste of the glory Christians will enjoy in the age to come. . . . Once we reach this state, we will know what the meaning of perfect love is—the love of God with all the heart, soul, and mind and love of neighbor as ourselves."[68]

---

67. Adam, *Edge of Glory*, 106–7, and *Holy Island of Lindisfarne*, 2–4.
68. Matthew the Poor, *Orthodox Prayer Life*, 112.

# Chapter 9

# Transfigured Character

Whoever does not love does not know God, because God is love.

—*1* John 4:8 NIV

The spiritual path is a journey towards perfection, the route to which is constant spiritual growth.

—**Pope Shenouda III,** *Spiritual Path*

Blessed be thine infinite mercy, who sentest thine own Son to dwell among men, and to instruct them by his example as well as his laws, giving them a perfect pattern of what they ought to be.

—**Henry Scougal,** *Life of God*

We actively manifest love in forbearance and patience towards our neighbour, in genuinely desiring his good, and in the right use of material things.

—**Maximos the Confessor, The** *Philokalia*

The one who is transfigured on the mountain is the one who is disfigured by anguish, pain and death on the cross. The two cannot be separated.

—**Dorothy Lee,** *Transfiguration*

JOHN OSWALT MAKES IT very clear that "Christians are to live lives which radically manifest the unique character of God."[1] Oswalt follows Wesley's sermon on "The New Birth," which draws the necessary connection between sanctification and love.[2] A life lived in the transforming power of

---

1. Oswalt, *Called to Be Holy*, 3.
2. Outler, *Works of John Wesley*, 2:186–201.

grace "results in inward change that manifests in righteous outward actions. The goal is change in the very nature of the believer, something that will bear fruit in outward behavior."[3] What is needed is a "transfigured moral life."[4] To live a life of this love towards all is "acting like our Father which is in heaven."[5]

The entire universe, God's pursuit of humanity, and the core and measure of ethics and values reveal a depth of love that surpasses sentimentality and brushes aside any idea that God is arbitrary or capricious. God's love is expressed in the Old Testament by the Hebrew word *hesed*, meaning not a passing disposition, but something infinitely deep, never-ending, overflowing, reliable, and powerful. To show how profound and distinctive this is, Oswalt points out that while *hesed* "occurs more than 240 times in the Hebrew Bible, it has no cognates in other Semitic languages."[6] John Wesley viewed love as God's "reigning attribute."[7] Craig Keener notes that "Although many ancient thinkers, especially among Jewish teachers, regarded love as an important virtue, Christians were the only movement where it was the chief virtue."[8] In Wesleyan theology,

> As we grow in sanctification, love increasingly comes to govern our hearts and motivates our lives. At the same time, inward sin decreases, becoming less of a factor in our lives. But we yearn for love to so fill our hearts that there is no longer room for sin. This is Christian perfection, in which we become fully restored to the image of God.[9]

The full demonstration of this love comes to us in Jesus Christ. "We love because he first loved us" (1 John 4:19 NIV). In fact, "God demonstrates his own love for us in this: While we were still sinners, Christ died for us" (Rom 5:8 NIV). We "know what love is" because we have seen it in his sacrificial love for us, which became the standard and motivation for pouring out our own lives for others (1 John 3:16 NIV). In other words, Jesus is the model and teacher for Christian behavior. As S. T. Kimbrough notes, "If we share God's holiness, our likeness mirrors God's holiness and

3. Long, *Quest for Holiness*, 86.

4. Medley, "Participation," in Kharlamov, *Theosis*, 2:244.

5. John Wesley, in Cragg, *Works of John Wesley*, 11:52.

6. Oswalt, *Called to Be Holy*, 35n6.

7. Wesley, *Explanatory Notes*, 914.

8. Keener and Walton, *Cultural Backgrounds*, commenting on Colossians 3:14, 2087.

9. Knight, *Anticipating Heaven Below*, 23.

love in all that we think and do."[10] John Fletcher said that love is "making our gracious heaven below, as it will make our glorious heaven above."[11]

The power to actually live according to that model and teaching comes not from within ourselves, as if we could will such a thing, but from the Holy Spirit. That power is given specifically to transform character, to renew the human heart: "It is power for living out the character of God, for treating people justly and rightly, for living lives that are whole because they are wholly God's."[12] Christ is the source of holiness, needed every moment of our lives. "For God does not give them a stock of holiness. But unless they receive a supply every moment, nothing but unholiness would remain."[13]

Dorothy Lee comments on the paradox of cross and glory in Christian character:

> The cross is the revelation of divine love and of the tragedy of sin and suffering in the world. Christians are summoned out of this tragedy to live the life of God. Eastern Orthodoxy refers to this dimension as "deification", following the language of 2 Peter where Christians are called to become "sharers in the divine nature" (2 Peter 1:4); in the West, the language is that of sanctification and holiness.[14]

Commenting on 1 John, B.F. Westcott said, "The love [bestowed on Christians by God] is not simply exhibited towards believers, but imparted to them. The divine love is, as it were, infused into them, so that it is their own, and becomes in them the source of a divine life." Thus "we are children of God, and so share His nature."[15] In this way, "The kingdom of God comes into this world through our personal transformation."[16]

Oswalt wants to avoid an individualistic or escapist spirituality, saying,

> the holiness which God expects of his people is behavioral, and it is a behavior which cuts right across the grain of life, touching every aspect of it, whether personal, social, moral, civil or religious.

10. Kimbrough, *Partakers of the Life Divine*, 71.

11. John Fletcher, in Knight, *Anticipating Heaven Below*, 11; see Knight on Charles Wesley's use of "heaven below" and similar expressions by other early Methodists, 10–13.

12. Oswalt, *Called to Be Holy*, 79.

13. John Wesley, in Chilcote and Collins, *Works of John Wesley*, 13:99.

14. Lee, *Transfiguration*, 130.

15. Westcott, *Epistles of St. John*, 95–96.

16. Egan, *Book of Hours*, 86.

When God calls his people to be holy as he is holy, he is not merely asking them to live lives exclusively dedicated to him. Neither is he asking them to be especially religious. Rather, he is calling them to share his unique character, one that will alter how they approach every aspect of their lives.[17]

The transfiguration does not carry us over and beyond the hard realities of life and discipleship, any more than it carried Jesus over and beyond the cross. Instead, it provides the vision and power to be all God created us to be here in this world—in Charles Wesley's words, reflecting on Jesus' own ministry, to live "'Twixt the mount and multitude."[18] Just a few verses past Luke's transfiguration story, we read that, "As the time approached for him to be taken up to heaven, Jesus resolutely set out for Jerusalem" (Luke 9:51 NIV; NKJV: "He steadfastly set His face to go to Jerusalem."). Just as the transfiguration propelled Jesus to the cross, our own transformation prepares and empowers us for our mission in the world. Through it God sends us "to serve the present age," even as he "fit[s] us for heaven."[19]

Charles Wesley captured the juxtaposition of transfiguration glory and purposeful suffering, saying: "In momentary majesty / My Saviour on the mount I see, / As on his dazzling throne, / But when the glorious God appears, / He still remains the man of tears, / And speaks of death alone."[20]

The transfiguration, for Jesus and his followers, both confronts and eventually triumphs over suffering. Michael Ramsey says "We are bidden to journey on to Calvary and there learn of the darkness and desolation which are the cost of the glory."[21] Rob Marshall notes that "the glorious scene was a temporary one and the road to suffering and the holy city had to be travelled first."[22] Yet the final word belongs to the glory experienced in the transfiguration. Just as in Hebrews Jesus "endured" the cross and its shame "for the joy set before him" (Heb 12:2 NIV), we must endure the painful realities of life even as we seek their transformation.[23] In the Synoptic Gospels, the transfiguration moves Jesus and his disciples first toward,

---

17. Oswalt, *Called to Be Holy*, 33.

18. Charles Wesley, in Chilcote, *Changed from Glory into Glory*, 27.

19. Charles Wesley, "A Charge to Keep I Have," *UM Hymnal* #413; Anon., "Away in a Manger," *United Methodist Hymnal* #217.

20. Charles Wesley, in Kimbrough, *Partakers of the Life Divine*, 119.

21. Michael Ramsey, in Marshall, *Transfiguration of Jesus*, 88.

22. Marshall, *Transfiguration of Jesus*, 90.

23. Michael Ramsey, in Marshall, *Transfiguration of Jesus*, 88.

then beyond the cross: "It is because of the Transfiguration story happening when and where it did that there is already hope for those who have faith in Jesus Christ."[24] Our ultimate hope is "the hope of glory," Christ within us, the glory seen by the disciples on that mountain (Col 1:27 NIV; 2 Pet 1:16–18) and through their relationship with him (John 1:14). Ramsey notes that this glory includes "the transformation of sufferings and circumstances."[25]

The final result of living the full reality of transformed existence is hope-filled endurance in "steadfast love" (Ps 107:1 NRSV; Rom 15:4, 13; Heb 12:1; Jas 1:2–4). "Perfect steadfastness," says says Sophrony Sakharov, "is the conclusive gift for eternity of God our Saviour."[26] Henry Knight says that for the Wesleys, "sanctification is about having heaven in our hearts in the present." What does that look like? "As we grow in sanctification, we seek for God to fill us with love, so that it governs both our hearts and lives."[27]

Matthew the Poor makes very clear the difference our sanctification makes in the midst of a fallen and hurting world:

> To live in the presence of God, conscious of the union with Christ that He freely accomplished in us and for us, is the secret of happiness provided by Christ for us amid the sorrows of the world and despite the helplessness of humanity and its tragic failure. This consciousness should give us an inner peace that transcends the mind with all its troubles and weaknesses."[28]

A transformed character includes a transformed perspective that sees life from the vantage point of eternity. In a prayer attributed to Pope Clement XI, we read,

> Teach me to realize
> how fragile this life is,
> How fleeting are the things of time,
> How great and lasting are the things that are eternal.[29]

Pope Shenouda wrote, "The spiritual life" of a transformed character "does not stop at a certain point. It is an unceasing walk, growing and

24. Marshall, *Transfiguration of Jesus*, 87.

25. Michael Ramsey, in Marshall, *Transfiguration of Jesus*, 88.

26. Sakharov, *We Shall See Him*, 60.

27. Knight, *Anticipating Heaven Below*, xii.

28. Matthew the Poor, *Communion of Love*, 162.

29. Quoted in Duffy, *Pilgrimage*, 124.

advancing at all times. Thus the life of growth is one of the characteristics of the spiritual path." This growth has a goal and direction, even if at times it seems to meander, fluctuate, or wander off course. That goal is "the perfection of your capabilities and the perfection of your conduct, until you return to the Divine image after which you were created." Like John Wesley, Shenouda saw that grace-empowered perfection could be gradual, yet recognized that "God is capable of uplifting you in one step, as He did in some of the saints." Like Wesley, he saw the principle of synergy: "At the same time in which you ask God to work within you, you also work with Him."[30]

Daniel Keating makes it clear that our transformation is not an escape from, or detour around, the hard work and even suffering that come with being a Christian. Keating says that while "Deification is a kind of summary term that expresses all that God intends for us in Christ through his Spirit," yet "deification is not a bypassing of the Cross or a passage to glory that avoids sharing in Christ's suffering and death. Because deification means being progressively conformed to the image of Christ, there is no route to this transformation apart from participation in the suffering, death, and resurrection of Christ."[31] As Matthew the Poor puts it, "it is impossible to share his glory without first sharing with him in his sufferings."[32] This was the reality first experienced by the disciples who followed Jesus down the Mount of Transfiguration and on to Jerusalem.

There is, says Pope Benedict XVI, "this intrinsic interconnectedness of Cross and glory" in the transfiguration.[33] Yet because of the transfiguration and Jesus' victory over sin and death, "a Christian asks God to transfigure the suffering and to lead him to the glory of the transfigured Jesus."[34] Glory strengthens us for the way of the cross, without removing us from it, but also carries us through and beyond it, to the place where evil and death are a distant memory (Rev 21).

Nor does our transformation exchange ordinary reality for the spectacular. Instead, the ordinary is infused with extraordinary power, purpose, and direction as "the believer discovers the indwelling glory of the divine character in the common pursuits of life."[35] At the same time, "Perfect

30. Shenouda III, *Characteristics of the Spiritual Path*, 258, 260, 265

31. Keating, *Deification and Grace*, 7, 87.

32. Matthew the Poor, *Orthodox Prayer Life*, 17.

33. Ratzinger, *Jesus of Nazareth*, 305.

34. Marshall, *Transfiguration of Jesus*, 89.

35. Bence, "John Wesley's Teleological Hermeneutic," 50.

love, the restoration of the divine image in humanity within history, is an anticipatory expression of the final restoration beyond history.[36]

Neither does spiritual transformation spare us the full reality of death as the necessary precursor to resurrection. Death, while ultimately defeated, remains our formidable "last enemy," which "must be destroyed."[37] In the words of an Orthodox Easter proclamation, "Christ is risen from the death, trampling down death by death!" But the death that is trampled and the death that tramples it are very real and tragic. The victory of Easter is not one against a trifling enemy, but one that "appears as something foreign, as unnatural, as fearsome and perverted."[38] Death, for Alexander Schmemann, is not to be treated superficially or obscured in euphemisms:

> Thus, death is the fruit of a life that is poisoned and perpetually disintegrating, a disintegration to which man has freely subjected himself. Not having life in himself, he has subjected himself to the world of death. . . . It is man who introduced death into the world, freely desiring life only for himself and in himself, cutting himself off from the source, the goal, and content of life—from God.[39]

Easter's full power, beauty, and rejoicing can only be experienced and understood when we face *this* enemy, in our own lives, in the lives of others, and especially on Good Friday, when we realize that Christ faced *this* enemy and conquered.

Nor does our transformation come easily, for it must overcome what Charles Wesley called "our bent to sinning."[40] As Thomas à Kempis put it, "We all have been born with a fierce, self-centered desire for success, status and pleasure that clashes with our longing for God. When one temptation or trial is over, another comes along, and we shall always have something to contend with, for we have lost the original happiness that God intended for us."[41] The conflict and struggle are real and powerful, but grace is equally real and more powerful.

The reason we can participate in this kind of transformation is God's transforming grace. Randy Maddox and Theodore Runyan talk about the

---

36. Oden, *John Wesley's Teachings*, 2:303–4.

37. 1 Corinthians 15:26; Schmemann, *O Death*, 24.

38. Schmemann, *O Death*, 30–31; Cf. Sakharov, *We Shall See Him*, 98–99.

39. Schmemann, *O Death*, 35.

40. Charles Wesley, "Come, Thou Long Expected Jesus," *United Methodist Hymnal*, #384.

41. à Kempis, *Imitation of Christ*, 41.

full range of meaning in this powerful term. Grace sets us free from our past, but it also empowers our future; grace "both communicates forgiveness and makes renewal possible."[42] This full range of meaning, rooted in the New Testament and Eastern theology, defines the Wesleys' theology of sanctifying grace. Wesley's theology of grace also incorporates the idea of synergy: "like his mentors among the Eastern Fathers, Wesley understands grace as co-operant. It invites into partnership. This partnership cannot be imposed but instead opens up a greater degree of human freedom." Theodore Runyan emphasizes this, saying that "Wesley's favorite quotation from Augustine makes the point plain: 'He that made us without ourselves, will not save us without ourselves.'"[43] It is that grace-empowered synergy that makes change possible, so that the new creation within us contributes to a new creation around us. All spiritual progress, beginning with repentance, "is a work of grace and not . . . the striving of the individual. It is a gift, not a discipline."[44]

Among those across the panorama of church history who have taken the call to holiness seriously are those engaged in the monastic life. From the Egyptian desert to the present, monks and nuns have walked away from the preoccupations and distractions of the world in order to pursue a life of holiness in the presence of God. In the Coptic tradition, desert monasticism continues today, often in monasteries tracing their roots back to the earliest days of the movement.[45] It is important to add that through prayer and active engagement, monastics have also demonstrated constructive interaction with the rest of the world. Reflecting on the life of the late medieval monk Thomas à Kempis, an important influence on John Wesley, William Creasy addresses the reason for Christian withdrawal, *and* the often unrecognized impact of life in the monastery:

> A monk, in the 15th century or now, directs all his energy, thought and prayer to preparing a room for God; it is his sole occupation, the focus of his life. It is his contribution toward rebuilding God's world on a foundation of love; though separated from it, he is intensely part of it. Others of us may participate more actively in the world, but we too should strive above all else to place God at the center of our lives. Following Jesus' example, we might teach and

42. Runyan, *New Creation*, 26; See Maddox, *Responsible Grace*, 23.

43. Runyan, *New Creation*, 30–31.

44. Matthew the Poor, *Communion of Love*, 87, 88.

45. Matthew the Poor, *Orthodox Prayer Life*; *Saint Anthony*; *Coptic Monasticism*.

heal and rebuild the world during the day, but at night we should retreat into the quiet of our own hearts for deep, intimate prayer; with God at the center, all we do will flow from him, and all we do will be for love of him."[46]

Monastics have influenced life outside the monastery in powerful ways. Adomnan, for example, from his base on Iona, negotiated a radical agreement among rulers and bishops concerning the conduct of war.[47] The community at Iona also initiated evangelistic forays into many parts of Britain and Ireland. These and many other examples shatter any idea of monastic vocation as escape. Their energetic involvement was rooted in the depth of their monastic experience. Monastics have been at the center of the theology and spirituality of transformation, and have adapted their insight and experience to the lives of ordinary Christians of many traditions.[48]

While monastic life in its various forms has been for some the ideal environment to "receive the gift of the Holy Spirit" and "save yourselves from this corrupt generation" (Acts 2:38, 40 NIV), others have sought to live the gospel within the world itself, while still separating for worship, prayer, and study. Such were the early followers of John and Charles Wesley.

For John Wesley, to live in love is to live in the character of God. Love is "the highest attribute of God, one in substance with the divine glory. If the objective of Christianity is knowledge of God and participation in the divine life, it must necessarily involve the pursuit of love." A life of practical, self-giving love is not a distraction from the spiritual path, but an essential part of it, one which mirrors Jesus' love for humanity and fulfills the Great Commandment. "Love is the highest perfection attainable this side of death."[49] But the reality and vision of love also extend beyond death. Pope Benedict XVI said in his first encyclical that love as we see it in 1 John 4 provides both "the Christian image of God and the resulting image of mankind and its destiny."[50] Nor is love "a mere 'command'; it is the response to the gift with which God draws near to us."[51] Charles Wesley expressed

46. à Kempis, *Imitation of Christ*, 27.

47. O'Loughlin, *Adomnan at Birr*; Wooding, *Adomnan of Iona*.

48. cf. Farag, *Balance of the Heart*; Shenouda III, *Characteristics of the Spiritual Path*; Boler and Cernera, *Contribution of Monastic Life*; Okholm, *Monk Habits for Everyday People*; Robinson, *Ancient Paths*.

49. Bence, "John Wesley's Teleological Hermeneutic," 56.

50. Benedict XVI, *God is Love*, 1.

51. Ibid., 2; Cf. Mantzaridis, *Deification of Man*, 61.

this connection between love and heaven in one of his best-known hymns: "anticipate your heaven below, and own that love is heaven."[52]

Kenneth Collins summarizes John Wesley's vision of transformed humanity: "Conformed to God's image in a superlative, translucent way, they shall radiate the divine glory throughout." Here we see the Christian's experience of "holy love" revealing "the shape of grace," but also the shape of a transfigured person.[53] This is the perfection of God's design for humanity, and of the restoration of that design in us. It must be lived out individually, as each of us walks a distinctive road to eternity.

> The spiritual life of every Christian has a specific rhythm or progression peculiar to him alone. But at the root of all that is the one Spirit [cf. I Cor. 12:4–11] and, consequently, the same ultimate purpose as contained in the commandments of Christ, summed up in the bidding, 'Be ye therefore perfect, even as your Father which is in heaven is perfect' [Matt. 5:48].[54]

Since Wesley saw love not just as one divine characteristic among many, but "His reigning attribute, the attribute that sheds an amiable glory on all His other perfections," love is obedience to an essential command and a powerful witness to Jesus' divine mission.[55] Love is the spiritual and practical working of grace in our everyday lives (Gal 5:6). Because "Love comes from God," we can know God and live in harmony with him as we receive and transmit his love (1 John 4:8, 19 NIV). Love is a participation in the character of the One whose image is being restored in us. To love in this life is an experience "limited only in degree, but not in kind, from that which is to come."[56] Transfiguration in Christ points us toward the everlasting kingdom and "participation in heaven changes life on earth: paradoxically, only otherworldliness guarantees proper engagement in this world."[57]

Wesley's view of love is echoed by Sophrony Sakharov: "In their essence, Christ's commandments [to love] are the self-revelation of God."[58]

---

52. Charles Wesley, "O For a Thousand Tongues to Sing," *United Methodist Hymnal*, #57, v. 7.

53. Collins, *Theology of John Wesley*, 325.

54. Sakharov, *We Shall See Him*, 62.

55. Wesley, *Explanatory Notes*, 914; Cf. John 15:12; 17:21.

56. Bence, "John Wesley's Teleological Hermeneutic," 55.

57. Boersma, *Heavenly Participation*, 5.

58. Sakharov, *We Shall See Him*, 72.

In his own way, Sakharov, like Wesley, makes clear the essential connection between love and the character of God:

> Divine love is the kernel of eternal Being. In it all the other attributes of Divinity—the Wisdom, the Kingdom, the Power, the Light—find their loftiest expression. It contains the beauty of the eternally unshakeable Kingdom. Christ's love is the revelation of the Mystery of the Father's love, too.[59]

God's love must be mirrored in us, so that as God's character becomes our own, we live out our lives' original purpose. God's commandments (to love God and neighbor) become internalized—an identity to live rather than laws to be obeyed. "And when these commandments, by His good providence, come to be the one and only principle of our whole being, both temporal and eternal, *then* we, too, 'shall be like Him; for we shall see him as he is [1 John 3:2]. GOD IS LOVE."[60] John continues his theme, saying, "Love is made complete among us" when "in this world we are like him" (1 John 4:17 NIV). The twin commandments connect heaven and earth and "holy eternity is contained in their spirit."[61]

Sarah Heaner Lancaster makes the same point, saying "Wesley carefully and intentionally describes the perfection that Christians seek in terms of love, loving God and loving neighbor. To be perfect as a Christian is to be holy, and to be holy as a Christian is to reflect God's holiness by loving as God loves."[62] Wesley elaborates his theology of love as it takes shape in a life of holiness in his "The Character of a Methodist" and his thirteen-sermon series "Upon our Lord's Sermon on the Mount."[63] Wesley walked squarely within the great tradition, expressed by John of Damascus, for whom "love is perfection defined."[64] The works of mercy, like the works of piety, "were means of grace used by God to grow in faith, hope, and love. That is, as we serve our neighbor, and as we pray, study Scripture, worship, attend the

---

59. Ibid., 147.

60. Ibid., 149, italics and caps his.

61. Ibid., 231.

62. Lancaster, "Soteriology and Eucharist," in Vickers, *Wesleyan Theology of the Eucharist*, 89.

63. John Wesley, "Character," in Emory, *Works of John Wesley*, 5:240–245; Outler, *Works of John Wesley*, 1:466–698.

64. John of Damascus, in McGuckin, *Transfiguration of Christ in Scripture*, 215.

Lord's Supper, and converse together, the Holy Spirit works to continue to transform our lives."[65]

People often ignore or reject the commandments to love God and neighbor as unwanted restrictions on their freedom and consequent happiness. They exchange what they see as "a kind of limitation imposed from without," for the path of "absolute self-affirmation, self-divinization."[66] Throwing off life in harmony with God, centered on God, humanity seeks its own way, only to discover that the road away from God "leads to death." (Prov 14:12 NIV) This is the sinful illusion that produced the fall. "Did not the 'temptation' described in the third chapter of the Book of Genesis mean exploiting man's natural aspiration to immutable eternity in order to instill in him the idea that his sought-for divinization might be achieved separately from this 'cruel' God?"[67]

Sanctification in Christ requires humility, a reflection of, and participation in, Christ's humility so clearly set forth in Philippians 2:5–11. "[Charles] Wesley knew that human beings are not the central focus of their existence. God is. The process of participation [in the divine nature] places God, the Holy Trinity, at the center. Hence, humility is requisite to its realization."[68] Humility surrenders any illusion of self-sufficiency or self-importance, providing an open heart for receiving and sharing God's transforming love. "We can begin acting as Jesus taught, not because of some titanic effort of will on our part, but because we have become different beings."[69]

In reality, the commandment to love is the commandment to be ourselves at our best, reflecting the One who created us: "In love lies [our] likeness to God who is love.[70] Love also leads to our destiny in Christ. Jesus describes the self-seeking alternative not as an imagined salvation, but the place of "weeping and gnashing of teeth" (Matt 13:42 NIV). Stated positively, in the words of A. M. Allchin,

> To speak of holiness in the Christian life . . . is to hint at unexpected capacities in human life, capacities which too often seem

65. Knight, *Anticipating Heaven Below*, 7.

66. Sakharov, *We Shall See Him*, 191.

67. Ibid., 213.

68. Kimbrough, *Partakers of the Life Divine*, 69; Cf. Fletcher, *Christian Perfection*, 113–99.

69. Casey, *Fully Human, Fully Divine*, vii.

70. Sakharov, *We Shall See Him*, 197.

to be almost wholly unrealized, but which spring to life once the Spirit of God touches the human spirit and sets it on fire with a divine longing.[71]

The biblical vision for perfection, holiness, or sanctification in this world is the highest imaginable: the holiness of God. In Leviticus 19:2, God speaks to Israel through Moses, saying, "Be holy, because I, the Lord your God, am holy." This is echoed in 1 Peter 1:15–16: "But just as he who called you is holy, so be holy in all you do; for it is written, 'Be holy, because I am holy'" (NIV). Jesus tells his followers: "Be perfect, therefore, as your heavenly Father is perfect" (Matt 5:48 NIV). For Paul, we must "become mature, attaining to the whole measure of the fullness of Christ," for our new selves are "created to be like God in true righteousness and holiness." (Eph 4:13, 24 NIV). Such a vision, if we take it seriously, can only prompt an astonished response like that of the disciples on the Mount of Transfiguration. Only by grace, in the power of the Spirit, could we even begin to imagine, or hope to be part of, such a transformation. Yet because of this grace, "Being a Christian entails living in and being transparent to God's glory."[72] Thus, in the words of the Coptic liturgy, we can pray, "grant us the Christian perfection that would be pleasing to you,"[73]

Galatians 5:22–23 famously pictures the Spirit-transformed character in this way: "The fruit of the Spirit is love, joy, peace, patience, kindness, goodness, faithfulness, gentleness and self-control" (NIV). Less famous is Paul's similar listing in Colossians 3:12–14:

> Therefore, as God's chosen people, holy and dearly loved, clothe yourselves with compassion, kindness, humility, gentleness, and patience. Bear with each other and forgive whatever grievances you may have against one another. Forgive as the Lord forgave you. And over all these virtues put on love, which binds them all together in perfect unity. (NIV)

Related lists in 1 Corinthians 13 and 2 Peter 1 add to these important descriptions of the difference a sanctified character should make in everyday life. Of course the New Testament also includes negative lists, such as "the acts of the flesh" in Galatians 5:19–21 (NIV), and the "old self with its practices" in Colossians 3:5–9 (NIV), which spell out in some detail what 1

71. Allchin, *Praise above All*, 75–76.

72. Chilcote, *Changed from Glory into Glory*, 9.

73. *Coptic Liturgy*, 15.

John 2:18 calls "the lust of the flesh, the lust of the eyes, and the pride of life"
RSV). Such lists can also be found beyond the New Testament, for example,
in the *Didache* (c. 100), with extended instructions on "the way of life,"
and a contrasting list describing "the way of death."[74] Still others appear in
early and medieval catalogues of Christian virtues and their correspond-
ing deadly sins, and in penitentiaries designed to remedy sinful behavior.[75]
What is essential here is what Jason Vickers calls "the healing and restor-
ative power of the Holy Spirit."[76] Transfiguration results not in fruitless
piety, but in the perfection envisioned in the Great Commandment. Like
the early Methodist movement, it was designed to "reform the continent,
and spread Scripture-holiness over these lands," creating "an evangelical
transformation of the world."[77] Transfiguration led Jesus to be "obedient to
death—even death on the cross!" and the God within us moves us to love
others by the same humility and compassion (Phil 2:8 NIV).

Thus, transfiguration is not escape, but empowerment. In the words
of Andreas Andreopoulos, "The vision of the divine light of God is not an
end in itself. As in the Transfiguration narrative, what inevitably follows
is the return to the world."[78] On the holy mountain, Peter understandably
expressed both confusion and a desire to capture and prolong the visionary
moment. "Rabbi, it is good for us to be here" (Mark 9:5 NIV). But as Luke
tells us, Peter "did not know what he was saying" (Luke 9:33 NIV). The road
would soon take them back down the mountain, back into the difficult and
confusing work of discipleship. It would take them to the glory of a resurrection they could not imagine, but not before it took them to the horror
and apparent hopelessness of the cross.

Hans Boersma calls life transformed by grace "heavenly participation," what Charles Wesley called "heaven below." Christians in this world
"participate in heavenly realities." so that "life on earth takes on a heavenly
dimension." Participation in heaven in this life does not remove us from
active involvement or render us no earthly good, but rather "changes life on
earth: paradoxically, only other worldliness guarantees proper engagement

74. Didache, in Richardson, *Early Christian Fathers*, 173.

75. Cf. the influential penitential of Columbanus in Davies and O'Loughlin, *Celtic Spirituality*, 246–56.

76. Vickers, *Minding the Good Ground*, 93.

77. Coke and Asbury, *Doctrines and Discipline*, iii; Bence, "John Wesley's Teleological Hermeneutic," 241; Cf. Jones, *Once and Future Wesleyan Movement*, 49, for a contemporary application.

78. Andreopoulos, *This Is My Beloved Son*, 105.

in this world." The world in eternal perspective invites and guides our constructive involvement, giving us more to offer than we could ever have as earthbound beings. "Precisely because heaven is already present on earth, the moral lives of Christians on earth are to reflect their heavenly participation."[79]

Each disciple is equipped to make a difference in the world, one that brings us closer to God's intent for our own lives and for all of creation. Using grace-empowered gifts for kingdom purposes is central to each person's "return to the world" from "mountain top" encounters. In view of the limitations of this quickly passing life, each of us is well advised to make the contribution that best fulfills our God-given purpose in life. Again, this is our choice, since "man has the power to disregard God and His will and to frustrate the purpose of his creation, although in doing so he forfeits the purpose of his existence."[80] Mantzaridis emphasizes the necessary synergy of grace and free will when he writes:

> Christ does not put an end to man's free will in the name of salva-
> tion, for this would involve a revision of the purpose of creation.
> Man was created free, and it was of his own will that he left God.
> This means that he can only continue to be man if he freely returns
> to God.[81]

There are opportunities for gifted participation for every personality and set of gifts. One example is the ministry of mentoring, in which mentors share the pilgrim journey with mentees in a mutuality where both experience significant spiritual growth toward wisdom, maturity, and destiny.[82] Billy Graham speaks of the need for older people to teach and model hope for younger generations. A large part of that special form of mentoring is maintaining a trajectory of spiritual growth that is contagious. "Take to heart what Peter wrote near the end of his life: 'But grow in the grace and knowledge of our Lord and Savior Jesus Christ' (2 Peter 3:18 [NIV]). In doing so, you help others do the same."[83]

Mentoring is one form of teaching ministry; another is writing, where the dimension of legacy can be especially clear and powerful. Christian involvement in the world can have an impact that far outlasts an individual's

79. Boersma, *Heavenly Participation*, 5–6.

80. Mantzaridis, *Deification of Man*, 22.

81. Ibid., 42.

82. Sellner, *Mentoring*, 138–41.

83. Graham, *Nearing Home*, 47.

lifetime. An ancient Egyptian monk named Theodore realized this as he wrote on a church wall in the Monastery of St. Anthony, near the Red Sea in Egypt, "The hand will perish, what is written will remain."[84] The Armenian writer Gregory of Narek sensed a similar need to leave a spiritual legacy as he sought to complete his book of prayers: "And although I shall die in the way of all mortals, may I be deemed to live through the continued existence of this book."[85]

Note that these words were written by Christians who had tasted eternal life in the midst of this life, and were looking forward to its fulfillment in God's kingdom. Yet they also knew their place in the generational relay race, the holy tradition they were passing along from God and from those who had come before, mediated by their own faith and experience. They looked beyond life's limitations, even as they felt them close at hand. Abraham Heschel wrote of this traditioning as "a link between ages" connecting past and present through our individual lives.[86] Knowing what is at stake in this, Ray Simpson warns that "a break in a living tradition of a land or a faith can kill it in a single generation."[87]

The real world in which we carry out our discipleship as part of our transformation can be frustrating, debilitating, and evil. Yet the balance always tips toward hope. The apostle Paul suffered beyond what most of us will have to face in fulfilling his own calling, yet he could say with absolute confidence in the same letter in which he details his experience of persecution, "Though our outer nature is wasting away, our inner nature is being renewed day by day" (2 Cor 4:16). Charles Wesley applied this thought to a different context in his hymn "For the One in a Declining State of Health," saying "The more the outward man decays, The inner feels Thy strengthening grace."[88] Strengthening grace makes all the difference as the Holy Spirit keeps renewing us, no matter where our journey may take us.

Sanctification is growth in love, love for God, and love for others—a living out of the Great Commandment. William Johnston, the medieval author of *The Cloud of Unknowing*, described the transformed character as contagious, even to the point where "His whole personality becomes so attractive that good people are honored and delighted to be in his company,

---

84. Mikhail and Moussa, *Christianity and Monasticism*, 329.

85. Narekatsi, *Speaking with God*, 641.

86. Abraham Heschel, in Sellner, *Mentoring*, 133.

87. Simpson, *Soul Friendship*, 71.

88. Charles Wesley, in Tyson, *Charles Wesley on Sanctification*, 240.

strengthened by the sense of God he radiates."[89] The love at the center of that character seeks the salvation of others, not just its own spiritual progress. Part of the outreach of sanctifying grace takes the form of heartfelt evangelism. Deification means that we reflect God's love and compassion for others, his will that all should be saved (1 Tim 2:4). "This supernatural desire for the salvation of others is in our will inasmuch as we enjoy a real participation in God's will."[90] The Great Commandment leads naturally to the Great Commission (Matt 28:16–20). Thus John Wesley conveyed to his preachers a desire for the salvation of all, which motivated the kind of sacrificial ministry that built the early Methodist movement. In a similar way, Johnston says, "Whoever wishes to follow Christ perfectly must also be willing to expend himself in the spiritual work of love for the salvation of all his brothers and sisters in the human family."[91]

Grace-empowered holiness reaches out to transform the world around us. Timothy Tennent calls this "missional holiness . . . a holiness that extends to the ends of the earth, encompassing all peoples and nations." Far from a life of isolated spirituality or legalism, "this viral, mobile holiness . . . sees the implications of holiness as both personal and corporate, both individual and systemic." The Spirit of Christ unites and energizes inward and outward transformation, from the depths of the soul to "the ends of the earth" (Acts 1:8 NIV). Scriptural "holiness is a positive vision of the full in-breaking of the New Creation."[92] This is why John Wesley saw holiness in terms of the Great Commandment, love of God *united with* love of neighbor.

In this, Wesley was extremely practical. The changes brought about by sanctifying grace represent a new life in Christ that is substantially different from the old one. They can be seen in

> love; joy; peace always abiding; by invariable *long-suffering*, patience, resignation; by *gentleness*, triumphing over all provocation; by *goodness*—mildness, sweetness, tenderness of spirit; by *fidelity*, simplicity, godly sincerity; by *meekness*, calmness, evenness of spirit; by *temperance*, not only in food and sleep, but in all things natural and spiritual.[93]

89. Johnston, *Cloud of Unknowing*, 117.

90. Michael G. Sirilla, in Hofer, *Divinization*, 101.

91. Johnston, *Cloud of Unknowing*, 82.

92. Tennent, *Call to Holiness*, 66, 67, 71.

93. John Wesley, "Farther Thoughts upon Christian Perfection," in Chilcote and

Such things described for Wesley a transformed character consistent with the character of God.

The early Wesleyan theologian John Fletcher spoke of Christian perfection as "a constellation" of constituent, "gracious stars."

> Christian perfection is a spiritual constellation made up of these gracious stars—perfect repentance, perfect faith, perfect humility, perfect meekness, perfect self-denial, perfect resignation, perfect hope, perfect charity for our visible enemies, as well as for our earthly relations; and, above all, perfect love for our invisible God, through the explicit knowledge of our Mediator Jesus Christ. And as this last star is always accompanied by all the others, . . . we frequently use, as St. John, the phrase "perfect love," instead of the word "perfection;" and understand by it the pure love of God, shed abroad in the heart of established believers by the Holy Ghost.[94]

Clearly, for Wesley, love is the essence and measure of God's presence in the life of a believer. So also for Luther: "The idea of a divine life in Christ who is really present in faith" produces "a consistent theology of love." Because God is love and Christ came to us in love at his incarnation, "we must once again break out through love to help our neighbor with good deeds, just as Christ became man to help us all."[95] Thus spiritual transformation is more than the legal fiction of purely judicial satisfaction and more than personal spiritual enhancement, for Christ empowers us to live his love in ways that change the world. By the power of strengthening grace, the Holy Spirit makes such a life imaginable and possible. Love is the measure and profile of Christian life in this world. "Therefore love is the fulfilment of the law" (Rom 13:10 NIV). "All the law and the prophets hang on" the twin commandments to love God and neighbor (Matt 22:40 NIV).

Old Testament prophets, who had experienced the Spirit's power themselves, spoke of a great outpouring of the Spirit in the lives of his people at a critical time in the future that would fulfill God's purpose. Through Ezekiel, God promised to "give them an undivided heart," one fully loyal to God and open to his leadership, "and put a new spirit in them; I will remove from them their heart of stone and give them a heart of flesh" (Ezek 11:19 NIV). Jeremiah described the human heart as "deceitful above all things

---

Collins, *Works of John Wesley*, 13:105, italics his.

94. Fletcher, *Perfection*, 9, 10.

95. Martin Luther in Mannermaa, "Why is Luther so Fascinating?," in Braaten and Jenson, 2–3; 13.

and beyond cure. Who can understand it" (Jer 17:9 NIV)? Yet God was not giving up on humanity. Instead, he was preparing to give us "hope and a future," in both the long and short terms. God's motivation: "I have loved you with an everlasting love . . ." His goal was a new covenant that would enable rebellious people to become "my people" (Jer 29:11; 31:33 NIV). In that new covenant, people who had been "without hope and without God in the world," are now "a chosen people" (Eph 2:12; 1 Pet 2:11, 9 NIV). "Once you were not a people, but now you are the people of God" (1 Pet 2:10 NIV).

Through Joel he promised to "pour out my Spirit on all people," so that "everyone who calls on the name of the Lord will be saved."[96] The deliverer of that promised gift would be the Messiah (Isa 44:2). The Holy Spirit came upon Jesus at his baptism and was active with Jesus throughout his ministry. Jesus promised the Spirit to his disciples and those who would follow (John 14:15–25; 16:7–15). He poured out the Spirit, as Joel had promised, on the Day of Pentecost, when his mission was launched "to the ends of the earth" (Acts 1:8 NIV).

Henry Scougal faced squarely the juxtaposition of God's power and the humanly impossible, knowing that even committed Christians would balk at the idea of attaining God's promised destination for their lives. He imagined such a person "like a man in a shipwreck, who discerns the land and envies the happiness of those who are there, but thinks it impossible for himself to get ashore."[97] Yet he answered this natural pessimism with two divine realities: the rescue mission of Christ and the empowerment of the Spirit:

> Did not the Son of God come down from the bosom of his Father and pitch his tabernacle amongst the sons of men that he might recover and propagate the divine life and restore the image of God in their souls?
>
> He hath sent out his Holy Spirit, whose sweet but powerful breathings are still moving up and down in the world to quicken and revive the souls of men, and awaken them unto the sense and feeling of those divine things for which they were made, and is ready to assist such weak and languishing creatures as we are in our essays towards holiness and felicity.[98]

96. Joel 2:28, 32 NIV; Cf. Oswalt, *Called to Be Holy*, 65–88.

97. Scougal, *Life of God*, 64.

98. Scougal, *Life of God*, 65–66.

Macarius the Great made a similar point: "The uprooting of sin and the evil that is so embedded in our sinning can be done only by divine power. . . . If, indeed, you could have done it on your own, what would have been the need for the coming of the Lord?[99] David Long says, "Every believer is called to imitate Jesus and be restored to his image. The beauty of this call is that he provides the power to make significant progress in that direction." This progressive transformation is not superficial, nor is it limited to certain compartments within us, for "every feature of one's life will experience change when we are being led by the Holy Spirit into the image of Christ."[100]

As John Oswalt has said, with the outpouring of the Spirit, the character and purpose of God—God's kingdom—would be known among and through his people. At two critical junctures in Jesus' ministry we are able to glimpse that kingdom—first at his baptism and later at his transfiguration. The two experiences are linked by the Father's voice from heaven:

"This is my Son, whom I love; with him I am well pleased." (Matt 3:17 NIV)

"This is my Son, whom I love; with him I am well pleased. Listen to him!" (Matt 17:5 NIV)[101]

In one of his sermons, Martin Luther powerfully describes the spiritual transformation that shapes Christian character:

And so we are filled with "all the fullness of God" [Ephesians 3:19]. This phrase . . . means that we are filled in all the ways in which God fills a man. We are filled with God, and He pours into us all His gifts and grace and fills us with His spirit [sic], who makes us courageous. He enlightens us with His light, His life lives in us, His beatitude makes us blessed, and His love causes love to arise in us. Put briefly, He fills us in order that everything that He is and everything He can do might be in us in all its fullness, and work powerfully."[102]

Alastair Minnis says of the reflections of Pseudo-Haimo on the Psalms, "The common material of the whole work is Christ . . . like wise (sic), the

99. Macarius, in Matthew the Poor, *Orthodox Prayer Life*, 130.

100. Long, *Quest for Holiness*, 68; 70.

101. Cf. parallel accounts in Mark and Luke.

102. Martin Luther, in Mannermaa, "Justification and Theosis," in Braaten and Jenson, *Union with Christ*, 35.

common intention is that it should make us like Christ."[103] Being like Christ means radiating the light we receive, for "the divine image shines inwardly and outwardly, so that others see the evidence of the transformation."[104] The identifiable content of that radiance is love, the highest motivation and goal of one who is seeking God.[105]

John Wesley had little patience with antinomianism, the idea that Christians need not concern themselves at all with works.[106] Works, when they arise from the love within us, are the necessary working out of our salvation and evidence of the sanctifying journey, "for it is God who works in you to will and to act in order to fulfill his good purpose" (Phil 2:13 NIV). By God's grace and with our willing cooperation, we can be "confident of this: that he who began a good work in you will carry it on to completion" (Phil 1:6 NIV).

Transformation in Christ, or *theosis,* does not isolate spirituality from character, but equips God's people to make a greater difference in the world. All of this is part of the exchange that frees us from debilitating sin and empowers us to be Christ's body as we interact with others. The result is not a choice between inspiration and action, but inspired action. For John Wesley, the reverse is also true, since action on behalf of, for example, the poor, is a means of grace.

> What takes place here between Christ and the believer is a communication of attributes or properties: Christ, the divine righteousness, truth, peace, joy, love, power, and life gives himself to the believer. At the same time, Christ "absorbs" the sin, death, and curse of the believer into himself. Because faith involves a real union with Christ and because Christ is the divine person, the believer does indeed participate in God. That is what Luther means when he speaks of Christ as a "gift."[107]

Recent studies of Luther's theology involving Finnish Lutheran and Eastern Orthodox theologians have found considerable depth in Luther's

---

103. Minnis, *Medieval Theories of Authorship,* 54.

104. Kimbrough, *Partakers of the Life Divine,* 133.

105. Johnston, *Cloud of Unknowing,* introduction; Cf. Bence, "John Wesley's Teleological Hermeneutic," 93, 107–13.

106. See John Wesley, "Farther Thoughts on Christian Perfection," in Chilcote and Collins, *Works of John Wesley,* 13:92–131.

107. Mannermaa, "Justification and Theosis," in Braaten and Jenson, *Union with Christ,* 32.

theology of justification, which goes well beyond any idea of salvation as transactional or forensic. For Tuomo Mannermaa, "Forgiveness and indwelling of God are inseparable in the person of Christ, who is present in faith. In that sense, in Luther's theology, justification and *theosis* as participation in God are also inseparable."[108] Risto Saarinen puts it in words that remind us of Wesley's theology of holiness, saying, "The Christian life can be described as follows: when the Christian has been justified, he takes a new road to deification, The church understands it to be a process of growing in holiness or coming closer and closer to God."[109]

For Charles Wesley, humility was an essential characteristic for anyone seeking radical transformation in Christ: "Thy nature doth itself impart / To every humble, longing heart."[110] That same humility caused him to emphasize sanctification, for most, as a long process. S. T. Kimbrough says, "sanctification for Charles Wesley is the Christian's lifelong pilgrimage—hence, it is a goal toward which one gradually moves throughout one's life. It is here that Charles stood at odds with his brother John, who desired to leave open the possibility of instantaneous or sudden sanctification." Yet Charles agreed with his brother that sanctification is desirable and possible in this life,[111] as John indicates here:

> God continually gives a considerable time for men to receive *light*, to grow in grace, to *do* and *suffer* his will, before they are either justified or sanctified. But he does not invariably adhere to this. Sometimes he "cuts short his work." [Cf. Rom. 9:13 –eds.] He does the work of many years in a few weeks—perhaps in a week, a day, an hour. He justifies, or sanctifies, both those who have *done* or *suffered* nothing, and those who have not had *time* for a gradual growth either in *light* or *grace*."[112]

Far from an onerous obligation, God's commandment to love is really an invitation to live in his Spirit, to joyfully reflect his character in our lives, as we walk the road of sanctifying grace. This is no path of outward

108. Mannermaa, "Justification and Theosis," in Braaten and Jenson, *Union with Christ*, 38.

109. Saarinen, "Salvation in the Lutheran-Orthodox Dialogue," in Braaten and Jenson, *Union with Christ*, 169.

110. Charles Wesley, in Kimbrough, *Partakers of the Life Divine*, 42; Cf. Andreopoulos, *This Is My Beloved Son*, 109.

111. Kimbrough, *Partakers of the Life Divine*, 122, 125.

112. John Wesley, "Farther Thoughts on Christian Perfection," in Chilcote and Collins, *Works of John Wesley*, 13:106, italics his.

obedience that leaves our inner selves untouched. Nor is it an inner journey that leaves our outward behavior untouched. Rather, it is the way of grace-empowered transformation that changes us from within and sends us into the world as new creatures in Christ. Salvation is not a superficial change in status, but a thorough, progressive transformation of character, defined by love. Heaven becomes a present experience, as well as a future promise. Discipleship is not a burden, but a gift, even when we encounter seemingly insurmountable obstacles along the way. Just as Jesus' transfiguration did not spare him from the cross, our own transfiguration does not protect us from the hard realities we will face. However, the promise of transfiguring glory is endless growth, ultimate victory, resurrection, and eternal life in God's kingdom. In this life and the next, we become more and more "like him," by the power of the Spirit (1 John 3:2 NIV; 2 Cor 3:17–18).

# Chapter 10

# Life and Eternity in Light of the Transfiguration

May God himself, the God of peace, sanctify you through and through. May your whole spirit, soul and body be kept blameless at the coming of our Lord Jesus Christ. The one who calls you is faithful, and he will do it.

—*1 Thess 5:23–24 NIV*

But our citizenship is in heaven. And we eagerly await a Savior from there, the Lord Jesus Christ, who . . . will transform our lowly bodies so that they will be like his glorious body.

—*Phil 3:20–21 NIV*

Grant us your light, O Lord, so that the darkness of our hearts may wholly pass away, and we may come at last to the light of Christ. For Christ is that morning star, who when the night of this world has passed, brings to his saints the promised light of life, and opens to them everlasting day.

—**Bede, in Duffy,** *The Heart*

Thee, Saviour, I my refuge make;
And when Thy nature I partake,
And all Thy fullness feel,
From fear, and sin, and sorrow free,
In perfect fellowship with Thee,
I shall forever dwell.

—**Charles Wesley,** *Charles Wesley on Sanctification*

The human race will one day be raised to the glory where He is.

—*Joint Commission of Churches in Turkey, Christianity*

THE MESSAGE OF CHRIST'S transfiguration and resurrection is that life and hope do not end at death. The resurrection was the foundation for early Christian preaching—"of first importance," as Paul said. So central was it that he could say, "if Christ has not been raised, our preaching is useless and so is your faith" (1 Cor 15:3; 14 NIV). Attempts to reimagine the resurrection as symbolic, mythological, imaginary, etc., fail to answer, for example, the formidable challenges of the apostle Paul in 1 Corinthians 15, or to explain the explosive history of early Christianity, and they leave all of us without hope beyond the confines of this life. Such attempts are both unconvincing and inconsistent with the apostolic witness.

Christians—indeed, anyone who treasures life and lives in hope—could never identify with the saying that appeared on many Roman tombs: "*Non fui, ui, non sum, non curo,*" or "I was not, I was, I am not, I don't care."[1] Death is not something to be welcomed or regarded with indifference or resignation. "The supreme evil here [the evil mentioned in the Lord's Prayer, from which we seek deliverance] is death itself, the final foe and gaunt presence behind all other enemies, from whom one must flee for protection to the Lord surrounded by his saints."[2]

The bodily resurrection of Christ, and his promise of resurrection to his followers, indicate both the importance of his mission, and the value God places on his human creatures. In his comprehensive study of the resurrection in its Mediterranean context, N. T. Wright has shown the uniqueness of Christianity's teaching on the resurrection of the body.[3] The resurrection is an unparalleled gift, not an invention or illusion. Countless writers and preachers have emphasized the radical, practical difference resurrection and eternal life make in the way we live, and in the way we look at our destiny in Christ.[4] Transformation demonstrates the power of resurrection.

The Old Testament's perspective, or rather perspectives, on death are mixed. At one extreme, for Psalm 39, hope is limited to this life and God's presence does little to prolong it: "I dwell with you as a foreigner, a stranger, as all my ancestors were. Look away from me, that I may enjoy life again before I depart and am no more" (Ps 39:12–13 NIV). Ecclesiastes recognizes that God has "set eternity in the human heart" (3:11 NIV), but

1. Russell, *Doctrine of Deification*, 29.
2. Ratzinger, *Eschatology*, 9.
3. Wright, *Resurrection of the Son of God*.
4. See, for example, Ryan, *Remember to Live!* and Vassiliadis, *Mystery of Death*.

that momentary glimpse fails to change the meaninglessness of life or the finality of death. Daniel offers a vision that will only be fully revealed in the New Testament, an end time when "Multitudes who sleep in the dust of the earth will awake: some to everlasting life, others to shame and everlasting contempt" (12:2 NIV). This word continues with a transfiguration-like promise: "Those who are wise will shine like the brightness of the heavens, and those who lead many to righteousness, like the stars for ever and ever."[5]

For Christians, Daniel's vision sharpens with the transfiguration and resurrection of Christ, and the New Testament's clear teaching about eternal life and the transforming power of grace. Justin Martyr's words reflect what became the early Christian consensus on human destiny when he said, "all human beings are deemed worthy of becoming gods and of having the power to become sons of the Most High."[6] Such a statement only makes sense in light of the Spirit's transforming power (2 Cor 3:18). Charles Wesley prays in one of his resurrection hymns that God will "*fill us with the Life Divine,*" that we may "*bear his nature to the skies.*"[7]

Of course, "Every one of us must *nolens volens* [whether we want to or not] suffer the mystery of death for the sake of becoming more like Christ. After we have crossed that still-unknown threshold, God our Father will lead us into the realm of eternal day."[8] It is that joyful promise that has always provided hope and motivated ministry in the face of death. In the words of pioneer circuit rider Jacob Young, "How gloomy and melancholy is old age, unless rendered cheerful by the hope of a better life to come!"[9]

One of the most exciting, encouraging aspects of God's transforming grace is its eternity and infinity. There is no end to spiritual growth and sanctification. Anthony Coniaris says, "Whatever state you reach there is literally an infinity of possibility for growth still before you. And according to the Fathers, this goes on for all eternity, even in the kingdom of God."[10] For "God is the infinite perfection, the endless ocean of all maturity, every beauty, every harmony, every wisdom and goodness." Thus the people of God will enter "ever more deeply into the ocean of the infinite perfection of God; they will always be moving from one wonder to another." This per-

5. Cf. Philippians 2:15–16; Russell, *Doctrine of Deification*, 52–57.

6. Russell, *Doctrine of Deification*, 99.

7. Charles Wesley, in Kimbrough, *Partakers of the Life Divine*, 44; italics his.

8. Sakharov, *We Shall See Him*, 41.

9. Young, *Itinerant Ohio Pioneer*, 277.

10. Coniaris, *Achieving Your Potential in Christ*, 14.

fection, as Vassiliadis indicates, is never static and never comes to an end. "That blessed life [in heaven] will never end and the righteous will live in it in the eternal light of divine glory."[11]

Further, eternal life is life in the communion of saints, fulfilling the experience of unity we experience as "one body" in the eucharistic fellowship (1 Cor 10:17 NIV). There will be joy in our eternal unity with Christ and in the fellowship of saints (Rom 8:17), fulfilling also Jesus' prayer for all believers, "that all of them may be one, Father, just as you are in me and I am in you" (John 17:21 NIV). It was John Chrysostom who said, "There we will not only recognize those known to us here, but also those we never saw before."[12] Nikolaos Vassiliadis believes that the disciples' recognition of Moses and Elijah on the Mount of Transfiguration prefigures our recognition of each other in eternity.[13]

> In reality then, we will not be deprived from knowing and seeing each other, for as we are going to enjoy the brightness and vision of the (divine) light more and more clearly, so also are we going to know and look upon God and upon each other with ever greater clarity, with inexpressible gladness and joy unto ages of ages.[14]

Early Methodist Bible scholar Adam Clarke envisioned eternal life as the place "where he [God] is seen AS HE IS; and where he can be enjoyed without interruption in an eternal progression of knowledge and beatitude." Transfigured in Christ, "The soul is renewed in glory; the body fashioned after the glorious human nature of Jesus Christ; and both joined together in an indestructible bond, clearer than the indestructible moon, brighter than the sun, and more resplendent than all the heavenly spheres." For Clarke, heaven transcends everything that now limits our spiritual growth. "From it all evil is absent, and in it all good is present." There will be "an eternal progression into the fullness of God," in which "every moment will open a new source of pleasure, instruction, and improvement."[15] And because God is both infinite and eternal, there will always be new spiritual riches to discover and enjoy in his limitless reality. This is the destiny for those who have traveled "the path of life" (Ps 16:11 NIV).

---

11. Vassiliadis, *Mystery of Death*, 556, 555.

12. Ibid., 564.

13. Ibid., 563.

14. Symeon the New Theologian, in Vassiliadis, *Mystery of Death*, 566.

15. Clarke, *Christian Theology*, 377, 378, 379; emphasis Clarke's.

This limitless, eternal kingdom extends beyond the individual and beyond humanity, for "the metamorphosis . . . extends to the whole creation. . . . The transfiguration is about the renewing and restoring of the earth."[16] It is this larger vision that takes shape in the last chapters of Revelation.

Because hope is both essential to human life and easily trivialized and misunderstood, the transfiguration and hope must be kept front and center in Christian thought, preaching, art, music, and symbolism. For example, the anchor, once a common emblem in sanctuary after sanctuary, has become a neglected symbol of hope. Carved in oak or pictured in stained glass, this early Christian symbol still appears, though largely unnoticed, in many older, and some newer churches. We find the anchor and hope connected in Hebrews 6:19: "We have this hope as an anchor for the soul, firm and secure" (NIV). The anchor also connects with the symbol of a sailing ship, representing the church in its voyage of salvation toward eternity. Rooted in God's purpose and promise, the hope expressed in these symbols transforms our lives and points to our destiny in Christ. Yet today the connection between symbol and reality has been largely forgotten.

Hope itself seems to have fallen from its original place in our hearts and minds. Christian hope is more than ordinary optimism, as in "I hope it's a nice day," or "I hope our team wins." Hope is a foundational attitude toward life, rooted not in chance or luck, or in confidence in human endeavor, but in God. Hope, like joy, can flourish even when life brings disappointment or trouble. Hope grows out of our trust in God and his vision for our lives, a vision of "hope and a future" (Jer 29:11 NIV). Hope extends to the height and depth of this life, and to the endless expanses of eternity. Nothing, no matter how devastating, can erase that kind of hope. It is rooted in God's intention for humanity, for each one of us, and for the universe, symbolized most powerfully by the transfiguration.[17]

As an undergraduate at The College at Brockport, I took encouragement from the State University of New York motto of the time, "Let each become all he is capable of being." It was not a theological statement, but it did embody the hope and promise of a relatively new form of higher education and spoke to the heart of our vocation as students. Actually, this motto was adapted from a longer statement by Thomas Carlyle, one that placed its hope within a mildly theological context:

16. Lee, *Transfiguration*, 134.
17. McGuckin, *Transfiguration of Christ in Scripture*, 133.

The great law of culture is: Let each become all that he was *created* capable of being: expand, if possible, to his full growth; resisting all impediments, casting off all foreign, especially all noxious adhesions; and showing himself at length in his own shape and stature, be these what they may."[18]

As Robert Louis Stevenson once said, "To become what we are capable of becoming is the only end of life."[19] It is the realization of the hope built into us. Hope is the driving force of life, the motivation behind all motivations. Apart from God's vision for life and eternity, time and space set boundaries to our hope. But the transfiguration of Christ, and in him our own transfigured destiny, provide visions of hope beyond those boundaries. To live in hope is to know in our own lives "*epktasis*, that eager looking forward, that constant growth of the human person into the fullness of God, that continual journey further on into the boundless, shoreless ocean of God's love."[20] In the light of Christ's transfiguration, "Each day is a day of growth."[21] Too often we have limited our hope to this life, this transient junction of space and time. But the hope God gives us, represented in the transfiguration, knows no such limits. Death and infirmity, while formidable foes, are already conquered.

The story and experience of the transfiguration is all about hope. In one sense, it tells us, as it told Peter, James, and John, something new about Jesus Christ. They were disciples of a teacher and Lord they only dimly understood. They had seen and heard amazing things from him, but there on the mountain they saw and heard much more. Also in that moment, they were confronted with something new about *themselves, their* future, *their* destiny in Christ.

For good reason, Dorothy Lee points out, "Christians in the East regard the transfiguration as central to the symbolism of the gospel, disclosing as much about themselves as about God."[22] In the words of Proclus of Constantinople (d. 446), "Christ the Lord was transfigured . . . so that he might reveal to us the transfiguration of our natures that is to come."[23] If we are to move beyond the shallow distractions of life, there must come a time

18. Carlyle, *Critical and Miscellaneous Essays*, 1:20–21, italics mine.

19. Robert Louis Stevenson, in Coniaris, *Achieving Your Potential in Christ*, 5.

20. Allchin, *Participation in God*, 60.

21. Edward Pusey, in Allchin, *Participation in God*, 60.

22. Lee, *Transfiguration*, 1.

23. McGuckin, *Transfiguration of Christ in Scripture*, 184.

when "The soul recognizes that the point of her existence is to be with God, in Him, in His eternity."[24]

That transformation reveals God's kingdom and the "cosmic salvation" that will restore not only God's people, but the universe itself.[25] This hope, this destiny, this promise, comes to us from the One who is *El Olam*, "The Eternal God," who in Christ is "the pioneer and perfecter of faith."[26]

> God of life and glory,
>
> your Son was revealed in splendor
>
> before he suffered death upon the cross;
>
> grant that we, beholding his majesty,
>
> may be strengthened to follow him
>
> and be changed into his likeness from glory to glory;
>
> for he lives and reigns with you and the Holy Spirit,
>
> one God now and for ever.[27]

This transformation includes but extends well beyond individual Christians to embrace the whole body of Christ. In the words of Ambrose Autpertus (d. c.779) in a homily on the transfiguration, "Yet in this transformation there is also demonstrated what the future condition of the church will be for the saints in the heavenly fatherland."[28]

C. S. Lewis's compelling vision, "The Weight of Glory," shows that transformation in Christ changes us and our approach to life itself. It reveals a depth of reality that revolutionizes our perception of, and attitude toward, other people, demonstrating once again the difference it makes for us to share something of God's eternal perspective:

> There are no *ordinary* people. You have never talked to a mere mortal. Nations, cultures, arts, civilization—these are mortal, and their life is to ours as the life of a gnat. . . . Next to the Blessed Sacrament itself, your neighbour is the holiest object presented to your senses. If he is your Christian neighbour he is holy in almost the same way, for in him also Christ *vere latitat*—the glorifier and the glorified, Glory Himself, is truly hidden.[29]

24. Sakharov, *We Shall See Him*, 68.

25. Andreopoulos, *Metamorphosis*, 148.

26. Walton and Keener, *Cultural Backgrounds*, 54; Hebrews 12:2 NIV.

27. *New Zealand Prayer Book*, 565.

28. McGuckin, *Transfiguration of Christ in Scripture*, 294.

29. Lewis, *Weight of Glory*, 15, italics his.

As we ponder the hope the transfiguration brings to our own lives and to those with whom we "live and move and have our being" (Acts 17:28 NIV), we do well to ask ourselves, in the words of Edwin Lewis: "What are mountaintops for any how except to save us from the restricted horizons of the plain? Once you have really *seen*, and know that you have seen, no blurring of the vision by the buffetings of life's lowland journeyings can take from you—or, at least, need take from you—the glory of that vision."[30]

> Remember me, my God, and lead me along the right path to your kingdom. Amen.[31]

> May we all be on our way
> Together to Grace-filled Paradise.[32]


> Then let me on the mountain top
> Behold thy open face,
> Where faith in sight is swallowed up,
> And prayer in endless praise.[33]

30. Lewis, *Christian Manifesto*, 112, italics his.

31. à Kempis, *Imitation of Christ*, 157.

32. Michael Sheehan, in Ni Riain, "Ag Criost, An Siol," 182.

33. Charles Wesley, in Hildebrandt and Beckerlegge, *Works of John Wesley*, 7:441

# Bibliography

Achtemeier, Paul J., ed. *Harper's Bible Dictionary*. San Francisco: Harper & Row, 1985.

Adam, David. *The Edge of Glory: Prayers in the Celtic Tradition*. Wilton, CT: Morehouse-Barlow, 1985.

———. *Encompassing God*. London: SPCK, 2014.

———. *Glimpses of Glory: Prayer for the Church Year* (Year C). London: Society for Promoting Christian Knowledge, 2000.

———. *The Holy Island of Lindisfarne*. Harrisburg, PA: Morehouse, 2009.

Adomnan of Iona. *Life of St Columba*. Translated by Richard Sharp. London: Penguin, 1995.

Agpeya. *(The Coptic Orthodox Psalter): The Seven Daily-prayers (Canonical Hours)*. Cairo: Mahabba, n.d.

Alfeyev, Hilarion. *Christ the Conqueror of Death: the Descent into Hades from an Orthodox Perspective*. Crestwood, NY: St. Vladimir's Seminary, 2009.

Allchin, A. M. *God's Presence Makes the World: The Celtic Vision through the Centuries in Wales*. London: Darton, Longman & Todd, 1997.

———. *The Kingdom of Love and Knowledge: The Encounter between Orthodoxy and the West*. New York: Seabury, 1982.

———. *Participation in God: A Forgotten Strand in Anglican Tradition*. Wilton, CT: Morehouse-Barlow, 1988.

———. *Praise above All: Discovering the Welsh Tradition*. Cardiff, UK: University of Wales Press, 1991.

———. *Songs to Her God: Spirituality of Ann Griffiths*. Cambridge, MA: Cowley, 1987.

Andreopoulos, Andreas. *Metamorphosis: The Transfiguration in Byzantine Theology and Iconography*. Yonkers, NY: St. Vladimir's Seminary, 2005.

———. *This Is My Beloved Son: The Transfiguration of Christ*. Brewster, MA: Paraclete, 2012.

Arzoumanian, Zaven. *Studies in Armenian Church: Origins, Doctrine, Worship*. Burbank, CA: Western Diocese of the Armenian Church, 2007.

Augustine. "On 1 John." In *Ancient Christian Commentary on Scripture, New Testament*, Vol. 11, edited by Gerald Bray, 195. Downers Grove, IL: InterVarsity, 2000.

Augustine, Daniela C. "Liturgy, *Theosis*, and the Renewal of the World." In *Toward a Pentecostal Theology of* Worship, edited by Lee Roy Martin, 165–85. Cleveland, TN: CPT, 2016.

Baker, Frank, ed. *Hymns for the Nativity of Our Lord, by Charles Wesley, M.A.* 1745. Reprint. Madison, NJ: Charles Wesley Society, 1991.

# Bibliography

Baker, Matthew. *T. F. Torrance and Eastern Orthodoxy: Theology in Reconciliation*. Eugene, OR: Wipf & Stock, 2015.

Bangs, Nathan. *The Necessity, Nature, and Fruits of Sanctification, In a Series of Letters to a Friend*. New York: Lane & Scott, 1851.

Barker, Kenneth, et al., eds. *Reflecting God Study Bible*. Grand Rapids: Zondervan, 2000.

Bence, Clarence. "John Wesley's Teleological Hermeneutic." PhD diss., Emory University, 1981.

Benedict XVI. *God is Love*. Vatican City: Libreria Editrice Vaticana, 2006.

Boersma, Hans. *Heavenly Participation: The Weaving of a Sacramental Tapestry*. Grand Rapids: Eerdmans, 2011.

Boler, Martin, and Anthony J. Cernera, eds. *The Contribution of Monastic Life to the Church and the World: Essays in Celebration of the Fiftieth Anniversary of Mount Saviour Monastery*. Fairfield, CT: Sacred Heart University Press, 2006.

Braaten, Carl E., and Robert W. Jenson, eds. *Union with Christ: The New Finnish Interpretation of Luther*. Grand Rapids: Eerdmans, 1998.

Bray, Gerald. *Ancient Christian Commentary on Scripture, New Testament*, Vol 7. Downers Grove, IL: InterVarsity, 1999.

———. *Ancient Christian Commentary on Scripture, New Testament*, Vol 11. Downers Grove, IL: InterVarsity, 2000.

Brock, Sebastian, ed. *St. Ephrem the Syrian, Hymns on Paradise*. Crestwood, NY: St. Vladimir's Seminary, 1990.

Brooks, Peter, ed. *Christian Spirituality: Essays in Honor of Gordon Rupp*. London: SCM, 1975.

Carlyle, Thomas. *Critical and Miscellaneous Essays, Volume 1*. Boston: James Munroe, 1839.

Casey, Michael. *Fully Human, Fully Divine: An Interactive Christology*. Liguori, MO: Liguori/Triumph, 2004.

———. *A Guide to Living in the Truth: Saint Benedict's Teaching on Humility*. Liguori, MO: Liguori/Triumph, 2001.

———. *The Road to Eternal Life: Reflections on the Prologue of Benedict's Rule*. Collegeville, MN: Liturgical, 2011.

Chilcote, Paul Wesley. *Changed from Glory into Glory: Wesleyan Prayer for Transformation*. Nashville: Upper Room, 2005.

Chilcote, Paul Wesley, and Kenneth J. Collins, eds. *The Works of John Wesley, vol. 13*. Doctrinal and Controversial Treatises II. Nashville: Abingdon, 2013.

Christensen, Michael J. "John Wesley: Christian Perfection as Faith Filled with the Energy of Love." In *Partakers of the Divine Nature: The History and Development of Deification in the Christian Traditions*, edited by Michael J. Christensen and Jeffrey A. Wittung, 219–29. Grand Rapids: Baker Academic, 2007.

Christensen, Michael J., and Jeffery A. Wittung, eds. *Partakers of the Divine Nature: The History and Development of Deification in the Christian Traditions*. Grand Rapids: Baker Academic, 2007.

Clarke, Adam. *Christian Theology*. Salem, OH: H. E. Schmul, 1976.

Clendenin, Daniel B. *Eastern Orthodox Christianity: A Western Perspective*. Grand Rapids: Baker Academic, 2003.

Coke, Thomas, and Francis Asbury. *The Doctrines and Discipline of the Methodist Episcopal Church in America*. Philadelphia: Henry Tuckniss, 1997.

# Bibliography

Cole, Charles C. *Lion of the Forest: James B. Finley, Frontier Reformer*. Lexington, KY: University Press of Kentucky, 1994.

Coleson, Joseph. *Be Holy: God's Invitation to Understand, Declare, and Experience Holiness*. Indianapolis: Wesleyan, 2008.

Collins, Kenneth J. *The Theology of John Wesley: Holy Love and the Shape of Grace*. Nashville: Abingdon, 2007.

Collins, Kenneth J., and Jason E. Vickers, eds. *The Sermons of John Wesley: A Collection for the Christian Journey*. Nashville: Abingdon, 2013.

Collins, Paul M. *Partaking in Divine Nature: Deification and Communion*. London, et al.: T. & T. Clark, 2010.

Colon-Emeric, Edgardo A. *Wesley, Aquinas, and Christian Perfection: An Ecumenical Dialogue*. Waco, TX: Baylor University Press, 2009.

Coniaris, Anthony. *Achieving Your Potential in Christ: Theosis*. Minneapolis: Light and Life, 1993.

———. *Tools for Theosis: Becoming God-like in Christ*. Minneapolis: Light and Life, 2014.

*The Coptic Liturgy: The Holy Kholagy*. (n.p.): Oxford, 2007.

Cragg, Gerald R., ed. *The Works of John Wesley*, Vol. 11. The Appeals to Men of Reason and Religion and Certain Related Open Letters. Nashville: Abingdon, 1989.

Cross, F. L., and E. A. Livingstone, eds. *The Oxford Dictionary of the Christian Church*. Oxford: Oxford University Press, 1974.

Dales, Douglas, ed. *Glory Descending: Michael Ramsey and His Writings*. Grand Rapids: Eerdmans, 2005.

Daley, Brian E. *The Hope of the Early Church: A Handbook of Patristic Eschatology*. Grand Rapids: Baker Academic, 2010.

Daley, Brian E., trans. *Light on the Mountain: Greek Patristic and Byzantine Homilies on the Transfiguration of the Lord*. Yonkers, NY: St. Vladimir's Seminary, 2013.

Davies, J. G. *Pilgrimage: Why?, Where?, How?* London: SCM, 1988.

Davies, Oliver, and Thomas O'Loughlin, eds. *Celtic Spirituality (The Classics of Western Spirituality)*. Mahwah, NJ: Paulist, 1999.

Davis, Stephen. *Coptic Christology in Practice: Incarnation and Divine Participation in Late Antique and Medieval Egypt*. Oxford: Oxford University Press, 2008.

Dorotheos of Gaza. *Discourses and Sayings*. Kalamazoo, MI: Cistercian, 1977.

Drewery, Ben. "Deification." In *Christian Spirituality: Essays in Honor of Gordon Rupp*, edited by Peter Brooks, 32–62. London: SCM, 1975.

Duffy, Eamon, ed. *The Heart in Pilgrimage: A Prayerbook for Catholic Christians*. London: Bloomsbury, 2013.

Dunning, H. Ray. *Reflecting the Divine Image: Christian Ethics in Wesleyan Perspective*. Downers Grove, IL: InterVarsity, 1998.

Dupre, Louis, and Don E. Saliers, eds. *Christian Spirituality: Post-Reformation and Modern*. New York: Crossroad, 1989.

Egan, Patricia Colling. *A Book of Hours: Meditations on the Traditional Christian Hours of Prayer*. Chesterton, IN: Conciliar, 2010.

el-Meskeen, Matta (Matthew the Poor). *Coptic Monasticism & The Monastery of St. Macarius: A Short History*. Cairo: Monastery of St. Macarius, 1984.

Emory, John, ed. *The Works of the Rev. John Wesley, A.M.*, Vol. 5. New York: T. Mason & G. Lane, 1839.

Ervine, Roberta R., ed. *Worship Traditions in Armenia and the Neighboring Christian East*. Crestwood, NY: St. Vladimir's Seminary/St. Nersess Armenian Seminary, 2006.

# Bibliography

Farag, Lois. *Balance of the Heart: Desert Spirituality for Twenty-First-Century Christians.* Eugene, OR: Cascade, 2012.

Farley, Lawrence. *Let Us Attend: A Journey through the Orthodox Divine Liturgy.* Chesterton, IN: Conciliar, 2007.

Finlan, Stephen, and Vladimir Kharlamov, eds. *Theosis: Deification in Christian Theology, Vol. 1.* Eugene, OR: Pickwick, 2006.

Fletcher, John. *Christian Perfection: Being an Extract from the Rev John Fletcher's Treatise on that Subject.* New York: Nelson & Phillips, n.d. (c. 1875).

Flew, R. Newton. *The Idea of Perfection in Christian Theology.* New York: Humanities, 1968.

Fry, Timothy, ed. *RB 1980: The Rule of St. Benedict.* Collegeville, MN: Liturgical, 1981.

Gause, Rufus Hollis. "The Lukan Transfiguration Account: Luke's Pre-Crucifixion Presentation of the Exalted Lord in the Glory of the Kingdom of God." PhD diss., Emory University, 1975.

George, Archimandrite. *Theosis: The True Purpose of Human Life.* Mount Athos, Greece: Holy Monastery of St. Gregorios, 2006.

Graham, Billy. *Nearing Home: Life, Faith, and Finishing Well.* Nashville: Thomas Nelson, 2011.

———. *Where I Am: Heaven, Eternity, and Our Life Beyond.* Nashville: Thomas Nelson, 2015.

Green, Joel B. *The Gospel of Luke.* Grand Rapids: Eerdmans, 1997.

Gregorios, Hieromonk. *The Divine Liturgy: A Commentary in the Light of the Fathers.* Mount Athos, Greece: Koutloumousiou Monastery, 2009.

Habets, Myk. "Reforming Theosis." In *Theosis: Deification in Christian Theology*, edited by Stephen Finlan and Vladimir Kharlamov, 146–67. Eugene, OR: Pickwick, 2006.

Habib, John. *Orthodox Afterlife: 2,000 Years of Afterlife Experiences of Orthodox Christians and a Biblical and Early Christian view of Heaven, Hell, and the Hereafter.* Sandia, TX: St. Mary and St. Moses Abbey, 2016.

Hallonsten, Gosta. "*Theosis* in Recent Research: A Renewal of Interest and a Need for Clarity." In *Partakers of the Divine Nature: The History and Development of Deification in the Christian Traditions*, edited by Michael J. Christensen and Jeffery Wittung, 281–93. Grand Rapids: Baker Academic, 2007.

Harink, Douglas. *1 & 2 Peter.* Brazos Theological Commentary on the Bible. Grand Rapids: Brazos, 2009.

Harper, Steve. *The Way to Heaven: The Gospel According to John Wesley.* Grand Rapids: Zondervan, 2003.

Heer, Ken. *Ancient Fire: The Power of Christian Rituals in Contemporary Worship.* Indianapolis: Wesleyan, 2010.

Hickman, Hoyt, ed. *The Faith We Sing.* Nashville: Abingdon, 2000.

Hildebrandt, Franz, and Oliver A. Beckerlegge, eds. *The Works of John Wesley, Vol. 7.* Nashville: Abingdon, 1983

Hofer, Andrew, ed. *Divinization: Becoming Icons of Christ through the Liturgy.* Chicago: Hillenbrand, 2015.

*The Holy Transfiguration: A Patristic Commentary to the Lectionary of the Coptic Orthodox Church of Alexandria.* Murrieta, CA: Saint Paul Brotherhood, 2014.

Hughes, Serge, trans. *Catherine of Genoa, Purgation and Purgatory, the Spiritual Dialogue.* Classics of Western Spirituality. Mahwah, NJ: Paulist, 1979.

# Bibliography

Humphrey, Edith M. *Grand Entrance: Worship on Earth as in Heaven.* Grand Rapids: Brazos, 2011.

Ignatius of Antioch. "The Letter of Ignatius, Bishop of Antioch to the Ephesians." In *Early Christian Fathers*, edited by Cyril Richardson, 87–93. New York: Macmillan, 1970.

Jenson, Robert W. *Ezekiel.* Brazos Theological Commentary on the Bible. Grand Rapids: Brazos, 2009.

Johnston, William, ed. *The Cloud of Unknowing and The Book of Privy Counseling.* New York: Image, 1973.

Joint Commission of Churches in Turkey. *Christianity: Fundamental Teachings.* Istanbul: The Bible Society in Turkey, 2017.

Jones, Scott J. *The Once and Future Wesleyan Movement.* Nashville: Abingdon, 2016.

———. *United Methodist Doctrine: The Extreme Center.* Nashville: Abingdon, 2002.

Kauflin, Bob. *Worship Matters: Leading Others to Encounter the Greatness of God.* Wheaton, IL: Crossway, 2008.

Keating, Daniel A. *Deification and Grace.* Naples, FL: Sapientia Press of Ave Maria University, 2007.

Keener, Craig S. *A Commentary on the Gospel of Matthew.* Grand Rapids: Eerdmans, 1999.

Keener, Craig S., and John H. Walton. *NIV Cultural Backgrounds Study Bible: Bringing to Life the Ancient World of Scripture.* Grand Rapids: Zondervan, 2016.

à Kempis, Thomas. *The Imitation of Christ.* Translated by William C. Creasy. Notre Dame: Ave Maria, 1989.

Kharlamov, Vladimir, ed. *Theosis: Deification in Christian Theology, Vol. 2.* Eugene, OR: Pickwick, 2011.

Khoo, Lorna. *Wesleyan Eucharistic Spirituality.* Adelaide, Australia: ATF, 2005.

Kimbrough, S. T. *Orthodox and Wesleyan Spirituality.* Crestwood, NY: St. Vladimir's, 2002.

———. *Partakers of the Life Divine: Participation in the Divine Nature in the Writings of Charles Wesley.* Eugene, OR: Cascade, 2016.

Knight, Hal (Henry). "To Spread Scripture Holiness over the Land." In Form of Discipline, no editor, iii. Philadelphia: R. Aitken & Son, 1790.

Knight, Henry. *Anticipating Heaven Below: Optimism of Grace from Wesley to the Pentecostals.* Eugene, OR: Cascade, 2014.

Lancaster, Sarah Heaner. "Soteriology and Eucharist." In A Wesleyan Theology of the Eucharist: The Presence of God for Christian Life and Ministry, edited by Jason Vickers, 87–99. Nashville: United Methodist General Board of Higher Education and Ministry, 2016.

Law, Willliam. *A Practical Treatise upon Christian Perfection.* London: Forgotten, 2016.

———. *A Serious Call to a Devout and Holy Life.* Grand Rapids: Eerdmans, 1966.

Leclerc, Diane. *Discovering Christian Holiness: The Heart of Wesleyan-Holiness Theology.* Kansas City: Beacon Hill, 2010.

Lee, Dorothy. *Transfiguration.* New York: Continuum, 2004.

Lewis, C. S. *The Weight of Glory and Other Addresses.* Grand Rapids: Eerdmans, 1949.

Lewis, Edwin. *A Christian Manifesto.* New York: Abingdon, 1934.

Long, David C. *The Quest for Holiness: From Shallow Belief to Mature Believer.* Franklin, TN: Seedbed, 2016.

Lossky, Vladimir. *In the Image and Likeness of God.* Crestwood, NY: St. Vladimir's Seminary, 1974.

———. *The Mystical Theology of the Eastern Church.* Crestwood, NY: St. Vladimir's Seminary, 1976.

# Bibliography

Maddox, Randy L. *Responsible Grace*. Nashville: Kingswood, 1994.

Maloney, George A., Ed. *Pseudo-Macarius: The Fifty Spiritual Homilies and the Great Letter*. New York: Paulist, 1992.

Manley, Johanna, ed. *The Bible and the Holy Fathers for Orthodox*. Menlo Park, CA: Monastery, 1990.

Mannermaa, Tuomo. "Justification and Theosis in Lutheran-Orthodox Perspective." In *Union with Christ: The New Finnish Interpretation of Luther*, edited by Carl E. Braaten and Robert W. Jensen, 25–41. Grand Rapids: Eerdmans, 1998.

———. "Why is Luther so Fascinating?" In *Union with Christ: The New Finnish Interpretation of Luther*, edited by Carl E. Braaten and Robert W. Jensen, 1–20. Grand Rapids: Eerdmans, 1998.

Mantzaridis, Georgios I. *The Deification of Man: Saint Gregory Palamas and the Orthodox Tradition*. Crestwood, NY: St. Vladimir's Seminary, 1984.

Marsden, George M. *Fundamentalism and American Culture*. 2nd ed. Oxford: Oxford University Press, 2006.

Marshall, I. Howard. *The Epistles of John*. Grand Rapids: Eerdmans, 1978.

Marshall, Rob. *The Transfiguration of Jesus*. London: Darton, Longman and Todd, 1994.

Martin, Lee Roy, ed. *Toward a Pentecostal Theology of Worship*. Cleveland, TN: CPT, 2016.

Mathewes-Green, Frederica. *The Jesus Prayer: The Ancient Desert Prayer that Tunes the Heart to God*. Brewster, MA: Paraclete, 2009.

Mathews, Edward G., Jr. "A First Glance at the Armenian *Prayers* Attributed to Surb Eprem Xorin Asorwoy." In *Worship Traditions in Armenia and the Neighboring Christian East*, edited by Roberta R. Ervine, 161–73. Crestwood, NY: St. Vladimir's Seminary and St. Nersess Armenian Seminary, 2006.

Matthew the Poor. *The Communion of Love*. Crestwood, NY: St. Vladimir's Seminary, 1984.

———. *The Monastery of St. Macarius: A Short History*. Cairo: Monastery of St. Macarius, 1984.

———. *Orthodox Prayer Life*. Crestwood, NY: St. Vladimir's Seminary, 2003.

———. *Saint Anthony: A Biblical Ascetic*. Sydney: St. Shenouda Monastery, 2014.

———. *The Titles of Christ*. Rollinsford, NH: Orthodox Research Institute, 2008.

———. *Words for Our Lives, Vol. 2*. Chesterton, IN: Ancient Faith, 2016.

———. *Words for Our Time, Vol. 1: The Spiritual Words of Matthew the Poor*. Chesterton, IN: Conciliar, 2012.

McGuckin, John Anthony. *The Book of Mystical Chapters*. Boston: Shambala, 2002.

———. *The Transfiguration of Christ in Scripture and Tradition*. Lewiston, NY: Edwin Mellen, 1986.

Medley, Mark S. "Participation in God: The Appropriation of Theosis by Contemporary Baptist Theologians." In *Theosis: Deification in Christian Theology*, edited by Vladimir Kharlamov, 205–46. Eugene, OR: Pickwick, 2011.

Meinardus, Otto F. A. *Two Thousand Years of Coptic Christianity*. Cairo: American University in Cairo Press, 1999.

Meyendorff, John. *Christ in Eastern Christian Thought*. Crestwood, NY: St. Vladimir's Seminary, 1975.

Mikhail, Maged S. A., and Mark Moussa, eds. *Christianity and Monasticism in Wadi al-Natrun*. Cairo: American University in Cairo Press, 2009.

Minnis, Alistair. *Medieval Theories of Authorship: Scholarly Literary Attitudes in the Later Middle Ages*. Philadelphia: University of Pennsylvania Press, 2009.

# Bibliography

A Monk of the Eastern Church. *Orthodox Spirituality: An Outline of the Orthodox Ascetical and Mystical Tradition.* 2nd ed. Crestwood, NY: St. Vladimir's Seminary, 1978.

Moo, Douglas J. *2 Peter, Jude.* The NIV Application Commentary. Grand Rapids: Zondervan, 1996.

Mulholland, M. Robert. *The Deeper Journey: The Spirituality of Discovering Your True Self.* Downers Grove, IL: InterVarsity, 2006.

Musurillo, Herbert, ed. *From Glory to Glory: Texts from Gregory of Nyssa's Mystical Writings.* Crestwood, NY: St. Vladimir's Seminary, 1979.

Narekatsi, Grigor (Narek, Gregory of). *Speaking with God from the Depths of the Heart.* Yerevan, Armenia: VEM, 2001.

Nellas, Panayiotis. *Deification in Christ: Orthodox Perspectives on the Nature of the Human Person.* Crestwood, NY: St. Vladimir's Seminary, 1987.

Newport, Kenneth G. C., and Ted A. Campbell, eds. *Charles Wesley: Life, Literature & Legacy.* Peterborough, UK: Epworth, 2007.

*A New Zealand Prayer Book.* San Francisco, CA: HarperSan Francisco, 1997.

Ni Riain, Noirin. "Ag Criost An Siol (To Christ be the Seed)." In *Treaures of Irish Christianity: People and Places, Images and Texts,* edited by Salvador Ryan and Brendan Leahy, 182–84. Dublin: Veritas, 2012.

Ochs, Phil. "When I'm Gone." *Phil Ochs in Concert.* New York & London: Elektra, 2004.

Oden, Thomas C. *John Wesley's Scriptural Christianity: A Plain Exposition of His Teaching on Christian Doctrine.* Grand Rapids: Zondervan, 1994.

———. *John Wesley's Teachings, Vol. 2: Christ and Salvation.* Grand Rapids: Zondervan, 2012.

———. *The Transforming Power of Grace.* Nashville: Abingdon, 1993.

Oden, Thomas C., and Leicester R. Longden, eds. *The Wesleyan Theological Heritage.* Grand Rapids: Zondervan, 1991.

Okholm, Dennis. *Monk Habits for Everyday People: Benedictine Spirituality for Protestants.* Grand Rapids: Brazos, 2007.

O'Loughlin, Thomas, ed. *Adomnan at Birr, AD 697: Essays in Commemoration of the Law of the Innocents.* Dublin: Four Courts, 2001.

O'Malley, Brendan, ed. *A Welsh Pilgrim's Manual.* Llandysul, Wales: Gomer, 1995.

Oswalt, John N. *Called to Be Holy.* Anderson, IN: Warner, 1999.

Outler, Albert C. "John Wesley's Interests in the Early Fathers of the Church." In *The Wesleyan Theological Heritage,* edited by Thomas C. Oden and Leicester R. Longden, 97–110. Grand Rapids: Zondervan, 1991.

———., ed. *The Works of John Wesley* 4 vols (1–4). Nashville: Abingdon, 1984–86.

Owens, Bernie. *More than You Could Ever Imagine.* Collegeville, MN: Liturgical, 2015.

Palamas, Gregory. *Gregory Palamas: The Triads.* Classics of Western Spirituality. Edited by John Meyendorff. Mahwah, NJ: Paulist, 1982.

Palmer, G. E. H., et al., eds. *The Philokalia, Vol. 2.* London: Faber & Faber, 1981.

Parsons, Elmer. "The Experience of Sanctifying Grace." In *Reflecting God Study Bible,* edited by Kenneth Barker, 871. Grand Rapids: Zondervan, 2000.

Payne, Richard J. *Catherine of Genoa: Purgation and Purgatory, the Spiritual Dialogue.* Mahwah, NJ: Paulist, 1979.

Payton, James R. *Light from the Christian East.* Downers Grove, IL: InterVarsity, 2007.

Peterson, Brent D. *Created to Worship: God's Invitation to Become Fully Human.* Kansas City: Beacon Hill, 2012.

Pierce, Timothy M. *Enthroned on Our Praise.* Nashville: B&H Academic, 2008.

# Bibliography

Pochin Mould, Daphne D. C. *Irish Pilgrimage*. New York: Devin-Adair, 1957.

Ramsey, Arthur Michael. *The Glory of God and the Transfiguration of Christ*. London: Longmans Green and Co., 1949.

Rattenbury, J. Ernest. *The Eucharistic Hymns of John and Charles Wesley*. Cleveland: OSL, 1990.

Ratzinger, Joseph. *Eschatology: Death and Eternal Life*. 2nd ed. Washington, DC: Catholic University of America Press, 2007.

———. *Jesus of Nazareth: From the Baptism in the Jordan to the Transfiguration*. New York: Doubleday, 2007.

Richardson, Cyril C., ed. *Early Christian Fathers*. New York: Macmillan, 1970.

*The Rituals of the Armenian Apostolic Church*. New York: Prelacy of the Armenian Apostolic Church in America, 1992.

Robinson, David. *Ancient Paths: Discover Christian Formation the Benedictine Way*. Brewster, MA: Paraclete, 2010.

Rowell, Geoffrey. "Michael Ramsey, Transfiguration and the Eastern Churches." In *Glory Descending: Michael Ramsey and His Writings*, edited by Douglas Dales et al., 188–210. Grand Rapids: Eerdmans, 2005.

Runyan, Theodore. *The New Creation: John Wesley's Theology Today*. Nashville: Abingdon, 1998.

Rupp, E. Gordon. *Last Things First: Four Lectures on Belief in... The Communion of Saints, the Forgiveness of Sins, the Resurrection of the Body and the Life Everlasting*. Philadelphia: Fortress, 1964.

Russell, Norman. *The Doctrine of Deification in the Greek Patristic Tradition*. Oxford: Oxford University Press, 2004.

———. *Fellow Workers with God: Orthodox Thinking on Theosis*. Crestwood, NY: St. Vladimir's Seminary, 2009.

Ryan, Salvador, and Brendan Leahy, eds. *Treasure of Irish Christianity: People and Places, Images and Texts*. Dublin: Veritas, 2012.

Ryan, Thomas. *Remember to Live! Embracing the Second Half of Life*. New York: Paulist, 2012.

Saarinen, Risto. "Salvation in the Lutheran-Orthodox Dialogue: A Comparative Perspective." In *Union with Christ: The New Finnish Interpretation of Luther*, edited by Carl E. Braaten and Robert W. Jensen, 167–81. Grand Rapids: Eerdmans, 1998.

Sakharov, Sophrony. *We Shall See Him as He Is*. Platina, CA: St. Herman of Alaska Brotherhood, 2012.

Samuelian, Thomas J., trans. *St. Grigor Narekatsi, Speaking with God from the Depths of the Heart: The Armenian Prayer Book of Gregory of Narek*. Yerevan, Armenia: Vem, 2001.

Sangster, W. E. *The Path to Perfection: An Examination and Restatement of John Wesley's Doctrine of Christian Perfection*. London: Hodder and Stoughton, 1943.

Schmemann, Alexander. *The Eucharist*. Crestwood, NY: St. Vladimir's Seminary, 1988.

———. *O Death, Where Is Thy Sting?* Crestwood, NY: St. Vladimir's Seminary, 2003.

Scougal, Henry. *The Life of God in the Soul of Man*. Edited by Winthrop S. Hudson. Mansfield Center, CT: Martino, 2010.

Sellner, Edward C. *Mentoring: The Ministry of Spiritual Kinship*. Notre Dame: Ave Maria, 1990.

Sheldrake, Philip, *Spaces for the Sacred*. Baltimore: Johns Hopkins University Press, 2001.

Shenouda III, Pope. *Characteristics of the Spiritual Path*. Cairo: Dar El Tibaa, 2000.

———. *Have You Seen the One I Love*. North Charleston, SC: BookSurge, 2008.

# Bibliography

————. "The Holy Transfiguration." In *The Holy Transfiguration: A Patristic Commentary to the Lectionary of the Coptic Orthodox Church*, no editor, 1–16. Murrieta, CA: Saint Paul Brotherhood, 2014.

Simpson, Ray. *Soul Friendship: Celtic Insights into Spiritual Mentoring*. London: Hodder & Stoughton, 1999.

Smith, Timothy. *Revivalism and Social Reform*. Baltimore: Johns Hopkins University Press, 1980.

Stevick, Daniel B. *The Altar's Fire: Charles Wesley's Hymns on the Lord's Supper, 1745 Introduction and Exposition*. Peterborough, UK: Epworth, 2004.

Stokes, Mack B. *Person to Person: Building a Relationship with God through Prayer*. Graham, NC: Plowpoint, 2007.

Sumption, Jonathan. *The Age of Pilgrimage: The Medieval Journey to God*. Mahwah, NJ: Paulist, 2003.

Sweet, Leonard. *I Am a Follower: The Way, Truth, and Life of Following Jesus*. Nashville: Thomas Nelson, 2012.

Taylor, Jeremy. *Holy Living and Holy Dying: Containing the Complete Duty of a Christian*. London: Forgotten, 2017.

Tennent, Timothy C. *The Call to Holiness: Pursuing the Heart of God for the Love of the World*. Franklin, TN: Seedbed, 2014.

Terian, Abraham, ed. *The Festal Works of St. Gregory of Narek: Annotated Translation of the Odes, Litanies, and Encomia*. Collegeville, MN: Liturgical, 2016.

Thompson, Andrew C. *The Means of Grace*. Franklin, TN: Seedbed, 2015.

Tuttle, Robert G., Jr. *Mysticism in the Wesleyan Tradition*. Grand Rapids: Zondervan, 1989.

Tyson, John. *Assist Me to Proclaim: The Life and Hymns of Charles Wesley*. Grand Rapids: Eerdmans, 2007.

————. *Charles Wesley: A Reader*. Oxford: Oxford University Press, 1989.

————. *Charles Wesley on Sanctification: A Biographical and Theological Study*. Grand Rapids: Francis Asbury, 1986.

————. *The Great Athanasius: An Introduction to His Life and Work*. Eugene, OR: Cascade, 2017.

*The United Methodist Hymnal*. Nashville: Abingdon, 1989.

Van Der Pas, Sarah, trans. *The Glossa Ordinaria—Epistles of St. John 1–3*. Consolamini Commentary Series. Monroe, LA: Consolamini, 2015.

Vassiliadis, Nikolaos P. *The Mystery of Death*. Athens, Greece: The Orthodox Brotherhood of Theologians, 1993.

Vickers, Jason E. *Minding the Good Ground*. Waco, TX: Baylor University Press, 2011.

Vickers, Jason, ed. *A Wesleyan Theology of the Eucharist: The Presence of God for Christian Life and Ministry*. Nashville: The United Methodist Church, 2016.

Wainwright, Geoffrey. *Eucharist and Eschatology*. Peterborough, UK: Epworth, 2003.

————. "'Our Elder Brethren Join': The Wesleys' Hymns on the Lord's Supper and the Patristic Revival in England." *Proceedings of the Charles Wesley Society* 1 (1994) 5–31.

Walker, Robert T., ed. *Thomas F. Torrance, Incarnation: The Person and Life of Christ*. Downers Grove, IL: InterVarsity Academic, 2008.

Walls, Jerry. *Heaven, Hell, and Purgatory: Rethinking the Things that Matter Most*. Grand Rapids: Brazos, 2015.

————. *Purgatory: The Logic of Total Transformation*. Oxford: Oxford University Press, 2011.

# Bibliography

Walton, John H., and Craig S. Keener. *NIV Cultural Backgrounds Study Bible*. Grand Rapids: Zondervan, 2016.

Ware, Kallistos. *The Orthodox Way*. Crestwood, NY: St. Vladimir's Seminary, 1995.

Warren, Rick. *The Purpose Driven Life*. Grand Rapids: Zondervan, 2002.

Watson, David F. *Scripture and the Life of God: Why the Bible Matters Today More than Ever*. Franklin, TN: Seedbed, 2017.

Watson, Kevin M. *The Class Meeting: Reclaiming a Forgotten (and Essential) Small Group Experience*. Wilmore, KY: Seedbed, 2014.

Watson, Richard. *A Biblical and Theological Dictionary*. New York: B. Waugh & T. Mason, 1832.

Weatherhead, Leslie. *The Transforming Friendship*. London: Epworth, 1932.

Wesley, Charles. "For One in a Declining State of Health." In *Charles Wesley on Sanctification*, edited by John R. Tyson, 240–41. Grand Rapids: Francis Asbury, 1986.

Wesley, Charles. *Hymns for the Nativity of Our Lord* (1745). Madison, NJ: Charles Wesley Society, 1991.

Wesley, John. *Explanatory Notes upon the New Testament*. London: Epworth, n.d.

———. *An Extract of the Christian's Pattern; or, A Treatise on the Imitation of Christ. Written in Latin by Thomas a Kempis*. New York: Carlton & Porter, n.d.

———. "Character." In *The Works of the Rev. John Wesley, A.M.*, Vol. 5, edited by John Emory, 240–45. New York: T. Mason & G. Lane, 1839.

Wesley, John, and Charles Wesley. *Hymns on the Lord's Supper With a Preface concerning The Christian Sacrament and Sacrifice. Extracted from Dr. BREVINT*. Bristol, UK: Felix Farley, 1745 (Reprint, Madison, NJ: Charles Wesley Society, 1995).

Westcott, B. F. *The Epistles of St. John*. Grand Rapids: Eerdmans, 1966.

Witherington, Ben III. *The Gospel of Mark: A Socio-Rhetorical Commentary*. Grand Rapids: Eerdmans, 2001.

———. *The Rest of Life: Rest, Play, Eating, Studying, Sex from a Kingdom Perspective*. Grand Rapids: Eerdmans, 2012.

———. *We Have Seen His Glory: A Vision of Kingdom Worship*. Grand Rapids: Eerdmans, 2010.

Wooding, Jonathan M., ed. *Adomnan of Iona: Theologian, Lawmaker, Peacemaker*. Dublin: Four Courts, 2010

Wright, J. Robert. *A Companion to Bede: A Reader's Commentary on The Ecclesiastical History of the English People*. Grand Rapids: Eerdmans, 2008.

Wright, N. T. *For All God's Worth*.

———. *The Resurrection of the Son of God*. Minneapolis: Fortress, 2003.

Youannis, Bishop. *Heaven: An Orthodox Christian Perspective*. Los Angeles: Saint Paul Brotherhood, 2010.

Young, Jacob. *An Itinerant Ohio Pioneer*. Cincinnati and New York: Cranston & Curts/ Hunt & Eaton, n.d.

Made in the USA
Middletown, DE
16 July 2021

44254026R00089